WORK LESS,
MAKE MORE

WORK LESS, MAKE MORE

Stop Working So Hard and Create the Life You Really Want!

JENNIFER WHITE

JOHN WILEY & SONS, INC.

New York · Chichester · Weinheim · Brisbane · Singapore · Toronto

Published by John Wiley & Sons, Inc.
Published simultaneously in Canada.

Work Less, Make More is trademarked by Jennifer White.

First published by Kendall/Hunt Publishing Company.

This publication is designed to provide accurate and authoritative information in regard to the subject matter covered. It is sold with the understanding that the publisher is not engaged in rendering legal, accounting, or other professional services. If legal advice or other expert assistance is required, the services of a competent professional person should be sought.

Designations used by companies to distinguish their products are often claimed by trademarks. In all instances where the author or publisher is aware of a claim, the product names appear in Initial Capital letters. Readers, however, should contact the appropriate companies for more complete information regarding trademarks and registration.

Library of Congress Cataloging-in-Publication Data:

White, Jennifer.
    Work less, make more : stop working so hard and create the life
you really want! / by Jennifer White.
        p. cm.
    Includes index.
    ISBN 0-471-35485-6 (alk. paper)
    1. Career changes. 2. Time management. 3. Wages. I. Title.
HF5384.W492   1999
    650.1—dc21   99-15650
                                                            CIP

10 9 8 7 6 5

For Steve, the man I love.

CONTENTS

CONTENTS

PART II
MAKE MORE   143

WORK LESS, MAKE MORE

INTRODUCTION

When people ask me what I do for a living, I usually answer, "I'm a success coach."

"A success coach?" they ask.

"Yeah, a success coach," I reply. "I help people to work less and make more."

More times than not they say, "Is it even *possible* to work less and make more?" (And they're thinking, "Yeah, right.")

It *is* possible to work less and make more. The book you're holding shows you exactly how to do it. The decision you need to make is whether you want to join me on this journey.

Many of you have put your lives on hold because you think you don't have the time or the money to make more of your life. You're full of reasons why your life isn't exactly what you want. Which one of these excuses fits your situation?

- If I just had more time.
- If I just had more money.
- As soon as my kids finish school.
- As soon as I get a new job.

- As soon as I get married.
- As soon as I get divorced.
- When I get promoted.
- When I get more organized.
- When the kids go to college.
- When my boss leaves.
- After my vacation.
- It's the slow season.
- It's the holiday season.
- When I find someone to. . . .
- When I get out of debt.
- When I get a better job.
- When my spouse.
- When my parents.
- As soon as I. . . .

Many people hold a secret belief that work has to be work and not any fun. They secretly believe that anything they *truly* want to do must go behind all their so-called priorities. They are too responsible to chase their ideas or passions. So those dreams that are burning in their souls are kept buried because they believe dreaming just isn't practical.

I know this probably rings true in your life as well.

What if the game you're playing simply isn't working anymore? You're stressed out. Burned out. Just plain tired. Yet you're not sure how to stop working so hard. You're probably afraid if you stop working, you'll end up broke and dissatisfied.

Deep inside, you may feel a great yearning. You're not quite sure what it is, but you think it's that you don't have enough.

- Not enough time.
- Not enough money.

So you begin pursuing them. You focus on external things—having a bigger house, a better car, a prestigious job. The feeling of emptiness may go away for a while, but it always comes back bigger and stronger than ever. That's why you don't take the time to celebrate your successes. You're still on the quest to fill in the hole.

After working with hundreds of clients, I know one of the reasons you keep your life so busy may be because you're afraid to address your inner issues. This doesn't apply to everyone, but it may explain why you aren't able to slow down. Why you're moving so fast.

You stay busy because you don't want to look at your relationships that aren't working. You stay busy because you don't want to address problems with your kids. Busy because you don't want to admit your career isn't satisfying. Busy because you don't want to face the fact that you've lost touch with the important people in your life. Most of all, you stay busy because you don't want to admit you have lost touch with yourself. And you're afraid that if you slowed down, the world would go on without you and what you did would not have mattered.

A consultant I know recently said it best. "I know if my desk is piled high with work and my calendar is full, I'm important. All the work proves it to me." Being so busy creates the illusion that you're someone important. Ultimately that busyness keeps you from truly living your life.

As long as you convince yourself that your work is so vital that it forces you to stay busy, you'll never reach ultimate fulfillment. You'll stop yourself from experiencing what life is all about.

The time has come for a new plan. A quest that is more achievable, more desirable and healthier than the old one. Where you must enjoy life to the fullest. Where you have plenty of time and money. Where you have the freedom to do whatever you want whenever you want. Where you find joy in your everyday activities. I call this journey Work Less, Make More™.

Work Less is not just about learning how to better manage your time. Yes, many of you want to spend less time at the office, and this book will help you do that. What Work Less also means is that you find so much joy in what you do every day that you come home from work energized and renewed rather than burned out and exhausted. Work Less is about putting the passion and inspiration back into your life. The problem is, most of you believe you don't have the time to make your life passionate again. This book will help you free up time so you can focus on living. Work Less not only means having the time to live the life you want, but turning your work into play so you no longer have to work at all.

The other part of this book is Make More. There's an important thing you need to know. Making more is not just about making more money. I know, that's probably what you thought when you read the title and bought this book. Making more is also about making more of your life. Isn't that why you want more time and more money? So you can have the freedom to do what you want to do when you want to do it. In other words, making more of your life.

Work Less, Make More is a lifestyle. It's about redesigning your life so you can feel satisfied. Fulfilled. Passionate about living again.

Working less and making more is a very personal quest to me because I spent many years working way too much. I was caught up in wearing the right clothes, driving the right car, having the right job, making the right amount of money. Isn't that what the American Dream is all about?

During those days—what my husband and I call the Dark Years—I spent a lot of time rushing around and not a lot of time laughing. I used to say, "If I had more time, I'd have more fun." The truth was I didn't have a clue what having fun was all about. I often found myself saying "Work is fun," but frankly, I was lying to myself.

You see, I was following the advice my parents, teachers, and mentors had given me. I know you've heard this advice as well. Some people call it the Puritan work ethic. What it comes down to is you must suffer and sacrifice for your success. You need to work long, hard hours, be fully dedicated and committed, and someday if you're lucky, success will be yours. I was determined to be one of the "lucky" ones. So I became consumed by my work.

I worked all the time. I was the one who turned on the lights at the office and the one to turn them off in the evening. I used to wake up in the middle of the night thinking about work. I talked about work. I thought about work all the time. I was obsessed with being successful. (My definition of *success* back then was "achieving at work.")

The day I decided to dramatically change my life was a day I'll never forget. I was with my husband eating pizza and drinking beer when out of the blue he said, "When are you quitting your job?"

I looked at him, shocked. "Why would I quit my job? I make great money. I have a company car. Free cellular service. A huge Rolodex. Besides, I'm too busy to quit my job. Who would pay the bills?" (Never mind that he owned a profitable company.) Notice what I focused on was all the stuff in my life. I was deeply concerned about what I had, not with who I was.

He calmly looked at me and said, "I don't like who you're becoming."

It was in that moment that I realized the person I was becoming was not the person I really am. My life was more than the money I made. It was more than the house I lived in, the car I drove, and the clothes I wore. On that fateful day, I decided to ask myself an important question, "How can I make more of my life?"

I went out to find the answer. I read books, and I went to seminars. I talked to successful people—wealthy people—and tried to figure out what they were doing. I found that many of them were looking for the answer to that same question. They weren't quite sure how to work less and make more, either.

I discovered that most people want to know how to find fulfillment and still have lots of money. I did, too. Living a simple life in the woods was not the answer. Work Less, Make More became my answer.

For me, I had to leave my corporate job and become an entrepreneur in order to start on my Work Less, Make More journey. But please know I struggled with this idea of working less and making more. Just because I quit my job didn't mean all of a sudden I got it. If you think I worked a lot when I was in corporate America, you should have seen me during the early years when I was in business for myself.

I learned how to work less and make more not only by experi-

5

menting with my own life, but, when I became a success coach five years ago, by learning a tremendous amount from my clients. I watched them struggle to work less and make more, and I was compelled to help them find an easier way. We worked together to find the path.

You'll meet many of my clients in this book who have done it. (I've changed their names to protect their privacy.) Many of them started in the same place you are right now. They wanted to work less and make more, but they weren't quite sure how to begin. You'll experience their pain and suffering. You'll see what they did to create new lives. You'll be amazed at their courage to dive in and change. And you'll learn exactly what they did with my coaching to work less and make more.

It is possible.

Now don't get me wrong. Work Less, Make More is not an easy program. It wasn't easy when I first started on this journey, and it's not always easy now. You'll need to take a good look at how you got to where you are right now. You'll need to decide what your life has been about up to this point. Inspecting your life with a fine-tooth comb is not an easy thing to do.

To be successful with Work Less, Make More, you'll have to make some hard decisions. Take some dramatic actions. Say no to some things that you want to say yes to. As your coach, I'll ask you to find a better way. Many times, it'll be a simpler way. And often you'll shatter your illusions and have to take a risk. It won't be easy, but if you're committed to working less and making more, you'll make that dream a reality.

This book helps you chart a course to make more out of your life. You won't find lasting satisfaction until you design a life that supports who you are, not what you have or do. Lasting fulfillment comes not from achieving and acquiring, but from becoming who you *really* are.

My vision for you is that you find deep fulfillment while making as much money as you've always wanted. I know you can make more of your life.

Get ready. You're about to embark on the adventure of a lifetime.

GETTING STARTED

There was a time, according to Hindu legend, when people had all the knowledge of the gods. Yet time and time again, they were more interested in pleasures of the flesh than they were in using the wisdom that was lying at their feet. (Times haven't changed much, have they?)

One day a god called Brahma decided to hide this wisdom where only the most persistent would discover it. He was tired of openly giving the people a gift they weren't using. And he knew if humans had to look for the answer, they would more wisely use it.

"Let's bury it deep in the earth," one god suggested.

Brahma replied, "No. Too many people will dig down into the earth and find it."

"Then let's put it in the deepest ocean," said another.

Brahma rejected that idea, too. "People will learn to dive and will find it someday," he said.

A third god asked, "Why don't we hide it on the highest mountain?"

Brahma answered, "No. People can climb the highest mountain. I have a better place. Let's hide it deep inside the people themselves. They'll never think to look in there."

So it was—and so it is.

You have all the wisdom, all the power, to start making more of your life right now. Problem is, you have all the knowledge, but you don't apply what you have already learned. Sure, there are things that get in your way. Every one of us has challenges that show up. I'll help you discover what those are so you can develop a plan to blast through your blocks. And blast through those blocks you will.

Before we go any further, it's important for you to know why this book is different. Why I'm different from most other writers you'll read. When I say I work as a success coach, I mean that I work with people just like you to help them become more successful. Often that means I help them create thriving businesses

7

or careers and still have a life. (Isn't that what we all want? Massive success and the ability to enjoy our lives?)

Sometimes I kick my clients in the butt when they need to get moving. And other times I'm the only one in their corner to support and believe in their dreams. I celebrate their successes, regroup after a mistake, and help them stay on track so they get to where they most want to be. To get there quicker and more easily, we all need someone to be accountable to on our quest for success.

My clients tell me I'm a cheerleader, sounding board, support system, mentor, consultant, and teammate all rolled into one. And that's what I want to be for you while you're reading this.

It's important to know that there are things in this book you may have heard before. Often, I'll remind you of the things you already know but haven't yet integrated into your life. That's the point of having a coach. You'll learn how to constantly improve your game, and often that means going back to the basics and re-learning, readjusting, and redesigning.

To have success, the key is to take what you're learning—or what you've learned before—and apply it to your life. Action is always the answer. Even if it's the wrong action, you're breaking your old patterns. And shattering your old patterns is a big part of learning how to work less and make more.

Always remember, no matter how great a coach I am, your success in Work Less, Make More comes down to one thing. You. When you're looking for the right answer, do what Brahma tells you: Look inside yourself. I can give you the tools to work less and make more, but you alone are the one responsible for your life. It's up to you to create the life of your dreams.

How to Use This Book

There are many ways to use this book. Some of you will want to go through this material alone. Just you, the book, a pen, and some paper. There are others who will form small groups—support groups in a sense—to help you apply the ideas and strategies. Some of you will call my office and ask us to help you find a coach trained in Work Less, Make More. You'll then hire a coach to create a system of accountability for you to ensure you're integrating these ideas into your life.

After watching—and coaching—hundreds of people through this process, I've decided the best way to read this book is to read it straight through the first time. (Yeah, you'll probably read this book more than once.) You'll notice that I divided Work Less, Make More into a 10-step process. Don't let the exercises in each section stop you from reading. Each step builds upon the other, and you need to get a sense of the entire process before you get down to redesigning how you work and live. The second time through, you'll want to make sure you do the work.

To make the most of the book, carve out at least 20 minutes a day to reflect on the ideas you're learning. At the end of each section, you'll find a wide array of exercises, tasks, and activities you'll want to do. My rule of thumb for the exercises is to do the ones that you resist the most. Only through pushing past your resistance can you find the truth. Remember, I said working less and making more requires that you shatter your old patterns. The best way to do that is to focus on the things that you resist the most.

Don't hinder your success by reading only what's in here. *Reading this book is not the same as doing the work.* The key is applying it. Integrating it. Using it.

What to Expect

Many people experience a tremendous amount of relief and then enthusiasm when they realize that it's possible to work less and make more. During the first few weeks, you may feel elated that you've discovered a new way to work and live. Keep in mind: The word *enthusiasm* derives from the Latin en + theos, which means "the god within." You're actually freeing the spirit within you to start designing the life you want to live. Honor your enthusiasm. It's a great feeling to know you can take back control of your life. You can.

That enthusiasm may soon be followed by annoyance, frustration, and anger. You may ask yourself why you waited so long to change. You may get downright mad at yourself for your past mistakes. Or you may get angry at other people for "forcing" you to live your life a certain way. This is part of the process. You're redesigning your life, and it's natural to feel angry. Just don't stop the process you've begun. The anger, too, will pass. It always does.

There are other times as you're working through this material when you're going to feel a little bit crazy. You'll be taking new actions, and you may feel frustrated because you're not getting results yet. Change takes time. Sometimes more time than you want. My advice: Just be patient.

Ah, there's that word *patience*. I always hated it when people told me to be patient. "For goodness sake," I always said. "There's so much to do. Who has time to wait?" I'm the type of person who used to hate waiting in lines. (Sometimes I still do.) I don't like to wait for people to call me back. I initiate follow-up phone calls all the time. I'm a take-action woman who didn't want to be patient. How boring.

That is until one day I realized that being patient doesn't mean you sit back and wait. Having patience is not about waiting, it's an *active* process. The story I'm about to share will show you what I mean.

One of my clients, Susan, had been building her consulting business for nine months. It had been a grueling experience for her. She had been talking with numerous prospects, yet none of them hired her. Time after time, Susan heard people say: "No, we're not interested in your services." "We don't have the money. Call us back in three months." "I just don't need a consultant right now." Her schedule was jam-packed with things to do, but the results weren't showing up. Susan was working more and making less, and she felt frazzled, frustrated, and upset.

She called me one day and said, "Jen, I think I'm going to get a part-time job. I just can't do this anymore. No one is interested in hiring me, and I can't figure out why. I've been at this for nine months, and it just isn't working."

I knew Susan's impatience was kicking in. In her heart, she wanted more than anything to be her own boss and to help people with her services. I asked her, "What do you still need to learn?"

The answer I got was silence.

We spent time exploring what she needed to learn. Susan agreed to take on some clients at a reduced rate to get more experience. Yet the most important thing Susan did was develop a daily routine she follows in order to be at her best every day, and she left space open on her calendar so she wasn't rushing around all the time. Most people in the same situation would have done one of two things: pushed and worked even harder or just given up. Susan took my advice and tried it a different way.

The lesson Susan needed to learn was that taking care of herself first was the answer to turning around her business. Before she developed a nurturing, less hectic routine, every time she met with prospects they could feel how anxious she was. Of course they didn't hire her. Who would? Susan needed to deeply nurture herself as her first priority every day, and only then could she concern herself with her business. She set out to learn the lesson rather than have "patience" to sit around and wait for her business to grow.

I knew she had learned what she needed to learn when she called and said, "I want to thank you. As you know, my business is going extremely well, and I feel as if I'm in the flow. Such a simple lesson to learn that took me a long time to get."

If you're not experiencing the results you want, perhaps, like Susan, you still have something left to learn. Or maybe you have something left to unlearn like an old behavior or way of thinking. Either way, take action, learn the lesson, and you'll find that your life suddenly leaps forward. It's funny, but life has a way of keeping us right where we are until we learn what we most need to learn. Then, voilà, everything changes.

When you begin to feel the roller-coaster ride of your emotions, use that as a signal to know you're growing. Changing and growing never take a straight course. It's messy, sometimes chaotic, and this up and down is part of the Work Less, Make More process.

I've seen many people give up and return to the lifestyle they had before when success was right around the corner. Don't let that be you. If you want to work less and make more, have confidence that the roller-coaster ride is part of the process. It's not a signal to abandon yourself and run away.

THE TOOLS YOU'LL NEED

Whenever I get ready to go on a trip to someplace new, I usually pick up the phone and talk with someone who's been where I'm going. I ask them all sorts of questions. What should I wear? Where are the best places to eat? What did they love or hate about that place?

I've had the experience of traveling down the Work Less, Make More path by myself and with hundreds of clients. And I have a few tips for you before you start your journey.

There are three key things you need to keep in mind as you're redesigning how you work and how you live. These three things are vital to having success with the Work Less, Make More program.

Please don't just flip over the next few pages. Take these recommendations to heart so you can get results fast. (Isn't that what we all want anyway? Yeah, I thought so.)

Your Support Team

A critical key to having success with this program is asking your family, friends, and close business associates to be on your support team. Before you begin to work, sit down with the people who are closest to you and let them know you're committed to Work Less, Make More. Tell them why you're embarking on this journey and what you hope it brings. Part of working less and making more means you'll have more time to spend with them. Explain that you need their support in the process of redesigning your life. You may even want to ask your support team to read this book so they can help you implement the ideas into your life.

Your business associates are especially important in this

process. A big part of working less and making more is redesigning how you work. You'll be experimenting with new ideas, strategies, and techniques. You'll be restructuring how you operate at the office, and your colleagues need to understand your motivation behind all the changes. Please do not surprise them with changes without letting them know why you're doing what you're doing.

Something crucial you need to know about your support team: Some of them may not be supportive at all. Think about it. You've been working hard for a few years now. Maybe a lot of years. You've been putting everything you have into your work, and the people around you are used to your being that way. They have grown comfortable with the way you are.

The sad fact is some of them will not be happy with the changes you want to make. They may even sabotage your efforts. A vital part of having success in this program is identifying who is part of your support team and who isn't.

Do not expect everyone to applaud your changes. That's like asking your drinking buddies at the bar to celebrate that you're no longer drinking. Some people in your life will become envious of the changes you're making because they wish they were the ones working less and making more. Other people will resent your newly found confidence that you can dramatically reduce your work hours and still make money. They may even try to make you feel guilty for redesigning your life. Just know that their guilt comes from their own fear of change.

Their comments usually go something like this: "Why don't you go out and get a real job?" "You are so lucky to have the life you have." "It's unfair how much you get paid for what you do." "Don't you feel guilty for asking for that much money?"

Be careful who you share your progress with. That's why the support team—not the sabotage team—is vital to your success. Only share your changes and your results with people who want to see you grow and expand. The only way to help your nonsupportive friends is to be a shining example of what their lives can be. Your change may become the message they need to hear.

A Journal

Buy yourself a journal—now. Your journal can be a spiral-bound notebook or it can be bound in leather. I've had clients who have made their own journals. It doesn't matter what type of journal you have. You just need something, anything, to capture your thoughts and feelings.

Your journal will soon become the gathering place for your good ideas. It allows you to capture *in your own handwriting* the experiences of your life. By keeping a journal, you're taking the time to learn from the past and the present so you can create a powerful future. A journal allows you to consciously chart the course of your life and capture the Work Less, Make More journey.

A big part of having success in this program is learning how to pay attention. That's one of the main reasons you're not working less and making more. You stopped listening to yourself, and you stopped paying attention. Your journal will become the critical link you need to live your life, not just pass through it.

I know some of you may be resisting a journal. First, for you males out there, you may be thinking journal writing is only for "girls." In fact, some of my clients who have received the most value from writing a journal are men. (And 80 percent of the clients I personally work with are men.) Set aside your feelings that journalling is just for women. It's for you, too.

There may be other resistance that's showing up for you based on nongender issues. One of my clients, Vickie, resisted the idea, too. Vickie works for a large company, and for the past two years, she's been trying to find a way to be passionate about her work. She has worked for the same company for 17 years, and the golden handcuffs were wrapped tightly around her wrists. Vickie felt as if she didn't have any choice but to suffer through until she could retire in 10 years. Until she decided to hire me.

I told Vickie keeping a journal was an important part of discovering who she was after working so hard all these years. I explained how much insight she would gain from writing in her journal every day, and I told her the passion she was looking for could be found in the pages of her journal. For weeks, Vickie told me she would write in her journal. For weeks, she didn't.

One day she came to our coaching session ecstatic. She had written in her journal three days that week, and she was shocked and amazed at what she had learned. By simply writing down how much she was resisting the changes in her life, Vickie was able to see what the truth was. Getting it down on paper allowed her to look at her situation with a new eye. From then on, her journal became the gateway to helping her discover her passion.

And rediscover her passion she did. Vickie decided to stay with her longtime employer and redesign how she operated. She moved to a new city, took a new job within the same company, and decided to "live large." Everything she does these days—both at work and in her life—is focused on getting the most out of life. Passion has become her middle name. All because she decided to write in her journal and discover what she wanted her life to truly be about.

Throughout this book, I ask you to write in your journal. Take the time to do the exercises in the back of each chapter. You'll discover that the answers you were looking for, those answers you never thought you'd have, suddenly show up.

Courage

Okay, I know what you're thinking. You're wondering if you even want to face all the work you have to do in order to Work Less, Make More. Perhaps you're even starting to feel frustrated that you can't just blink your eyes, and everything will change.

Guess what? It's your fear talking.

Fear is a powerful reason why you don't Work Less, Make More. You're very familiar with fear. We all are. It's your old friend, who tends to raise its ugly head right when you're at the threshold of success.

How do you overcome your fear and make the changes you want to make? That's a good question. Most of the time, the reason you don't work less and make more is simple: *You feel safer that way.* You may not be happy, but at least you're comfortable being unhappy. Much of what holds you back is fear of the unknown. You stay stuck because you're afraid. Yes, afraid.

You always have two choices when you feel fear. You can blast through it or you can stay stuck. It's your choice. The only thing I can tell you is to embrace your fear. There's another tool you'll need for this game. Plain and simple, it's called *courage*. A big part of overcoming your fear is learning how to embrace it. It's about facing your insecurities head on. Facing your vulnerabilities. And taking action in spite of the fear. You'll need courage to do all that.

Susan Jeffers wrote a book titled *Feel the Fear and Do It Anyway*. That's a powerful way to live your life. To live a life where you're working less and making more, you must have courage. You must decide the way you've been living is not working anymore. You must decide today's the day you're going to try it another way. Part of trying it a new way is taking risk. Experimenting. Discovering a new path. And having courage to do it.

I'd like to share with you a powerful poem that touched my heart when I read it. It reminds me that taking risks is the only way you can design the life you really want.

To Risk
To laugh is to risk appearing the fool.
To weep is to risk appearing sentimental.
To reach out to another is to risk involvement.
To express feelings is to risk exposing your true self.
To place ideas and dreams before a crowd is to risk their
   loss.
To love is to risk being loved in return.
To live is to risk dying.
To try is to risk failure.
But risks must be taken because the greatest hazard in life is
   to risk nothing.
The person who asks nothing, does nothing, has nothing
   and is nothing.
They may avoid suffering and sorrow, but they
Cannot learn, feel, change, grow, love, live.

Chained by their attitudes, they are slaves.
They have forfeited their freedom.
Only a person who risks is free.

—*Anonymous*

I want you to reach down into the essence of your being and find the courage to risk. Learning how to work less and make more will require courage. You'll have to ask yourself some important questions. You'll need courage to find the answers. You'll have to make choices, and you'll need courage to take the right steps.

The reason most of you are reading this book is simple. You want more freedom in your life. Take out a piece of paper and write "Only a person who risks is free." Put the book down and do it right now. Write it 10 times, then write it out in crayon or marker, and put it where you can see it every day. Only a person who risks is free.

I know you can do it. Turn the page and let's get on our way.

Exercises

1. Go out to the local bookstore or paper-supply store and buy yourself a journal. Write your name, the year, and date you're beginning the Work Less, Make More journey in the front of the journal.

2. Take out your pen and write your first journal entry. Ask yourself the question, "What does less look like to me right now?" Write for at least three pages. No more, no less. Just fill up three pages describing what less looks like to you.

3. Now ask yourself the question, "What does more look like to me right now?" Write in your journal for at least three pages. No more, no less. Just fill up three pages describing what more looks like to you.

4. Fear is a powerful motivator. Pull out a box of crayons, colored pencils, or markers. Take a blank piece of paper and draw what your fear looks like. Capture the personality of the fear that stops you from moving forward. Is the fear larger than you? Smaller than you? What color is it? What expression does fear have? Draw what the fear looks like. Don't worry—you don't have to be a Picasso. This drawing is only for you. Draw as if you're going to throw away the drawing as soon as it's done.

5. Now take the drawing you just made. Look fear straight in the face, then burn the paper. (Be sure you're in a safe place before you burn it.) Some people prefer to bury their fear in the backyard or flush it down the toilet. Just get that fear out of your life. Embrace how it feels to be fearless.

6. Pull out your journal and answer this question, "How is my life not the way I want it?" Be as specific as possible on what went wrong. Look at your relationships, money, work, opportunities, happiness, spirituality, environment. Where did you make a wrong turn?

7. Take a hard look at the people around you. Who wants you to change by working less and making more? What do they have to gain by your changes? What about those folks who will resist your changes? What do they have to lose?

Part I

WORK LESS

Work Less, Make More has nothing to do with looking at your weaknesses, and it has nothing to do with balancing out your skills. It has to do with focusing on what's brilliant about you. What you shine at doing.

CHAPTER 1

Uncover What Stops You

I know, you have many reasons why you're not working less and making more. After all these years of working with this material, I've heard every excuse imaginable. No matter who you are and what situation you're in, there's one thing that blocks you.

No, it's not the economy. It's not your boss. It's not your business. It's not your customers. It's not the government. It's not your employees. It's not your mother or your father. It's not your kids. It's not your neighbors. It all comes down to one thing: you.

You are the one who blocks your own success. I know, that's a hard pill to swallow. And I know that sometimes you want to blame your busyness, your lack of money, and your dissatisfaction with life on someone else. You can't.

In order to Work Less, Make More, you must take responsibility for everything in your life. You decided to be where you are today, and you're the only one who can change it. The key to working less and making more is clearly seeing what's blocking you so you can overcome it.

Imagine you're about to embark on a journey of climbing a mountain. That mountain represents your success. Before you start to climb, we need to evaluate what's in your backpack. It looks heavy. All the stuff that's in there is what you've used to become successful so far. (Or for some of you, all the stuff that's prevented you from being successful so far.) The problem is the world has changed dramatically, but you're still holding on to what used to work. Many of those old beliefs and behaviors weigh you down, and they will stop you from getting to the top.

Before you start the climb, do some unpacking and rearranging. In other words, you need to evaluate what's blocking you from having the life you want.

This chapter is full of evaluations and quizzes to help you identify what blocks you from working less and making more. Get out a pen, and be brutally honest with yourself. It's time to uncover the truth.

WHAT'S STOPPING YOUR SUCCESS

Once you can identify the reasons that prevent you from working less and making more, you'll be able to develop a plan to change your thoughts and your beliefs. Soon you'll change your behavior as well.

As you read the list on the facing page, put a check mark next to each item that applies to you. I've divided the blocks into two sections. The first section focuses on the reasons you don't work less. The second section focuses on why you aren't making more. Use the list to keep track of all the things that get in your way.

As you read the list, you'll notice that some items are big blocks for you. Others are annoyances. *Mark everything that applies, using a B for "block," an A for "annoyance."*

After each item, there's a number or numbers. These correspond to the chapter(s) in this book that deal with each issue. When you finish your responses, analyze them. See which chapters cover most of your major blocks and flip to them first. Read, learn, and take action. You can create your own path to working less and making more by blasting through what holds you back.

What Blocks Me from Working Less

_____ There's simply too much work to do. And I try to do it all. (3, 4, 5)

_____ I'm surrounded by clutter, and I can't find a thing. (5)

_____ I need to make money, and I think if I reduce the number of hours I work, I'll lose money. (3, 8)

_____ I get paid exchanging time for money. (2, 6)

_____ I am unable to say no. (5)

_____ I take on too many things. (3, 4, 5)

_____ My boss won't let me take more time off. (4, 7)

_____ I won't let myself take more time off because then the work simply won't get done. (3, 4, 7)

_____ I work with unqualified people who waste my time. (4, 10)

_____ I think if I say no, I'll get fired by my boss or my customers. (5)

_____ I spend too much time in useless meetings. (3, 4)

_____ I'm unable to relax, and/or I feel uncomfortable relaxing. So I don't. (5)

_____ I'm too busy accomplishing things to give myself time to breathe. (4)

_____ I procrastinate so I have to rush at the last minute. And I believe I do my best work under pressure. (4)

_____ I abandon my plans too quickly. When something goes wrong, I dump the plan and react to what's coming at me. (4)

_____ I won't delegate because no one can do the job to my standards. (3)

(Continued)

25

What Blocks Me from Working Less *(Continued)*

_____ I think if I'm not running around being extremely busy, I'm not successful. (3, 4)

_____ I haven't taken the time to automate part of my work. I know I should use my computer more, but I don't have time to set up the systems. (4, 6)

_____ I don't give myself time to sit and think, to come up with my own answers. (4, 5, 8)

_____ Technology (phone, faxes, e-mail) forces me to respond quickly to everything. (4)

_____ I'm afraid to try it another way. (Introduction)

_____ I feel guilty if I say no. (5)

_____ I feel guilty if I'm not working hard. (5)

_____ I think I don't deserve a better lifestyle. (1)

_____ I've tried to work less before, and it didn't work. (1)

_____ I have no idea what working less looks like. I'm too busy to focus on that. (3, 4)

_____ I feel like I need to compete with others as to who works the most hours. The one who works the most gets promoted or gets the big project. (2, 7)

_____ I feel guilty when I stop working, and there's still a ton to get done. (4, 5)

_____ I spend too much time watching television or playing on the Internet and then I get behind on my work. (4)

_____ I feel awful if I stop working to do other things. (4)

_____ Your reason _____

What Blocks Me from Making More Money

_____ I believe I'm making as much as I can. I've tapped out the market. (8)

_____ I don't think I'm worth more than what I'm already making. (1)

_____ I don't ask for more money. (7, 9)

_____ I'm afraid to ask for more. (1)

_____ I've been taught not to toot my own horn. So I don't. (7)

_____ I don't want to move outside my comfort zone. (1)

_____ I'm afraid I'll be rejected if I ask for more money. (1)

_____ I think in order to make more, I have to make big changes in my life. And I'm just not ready. (4)

_____ I believe that if I work hard, my employer or my customers will take care of me. (2)

_____ I get paid exchanging time for money. (6, 9)

_____ I think I'm worth only a certain amount of money each year. (1)

_____ I don't need more money. (1)

_____ Money is not the key to happiness, so I don't focus on money. (1)

_____ I don't take responsibility for my results. They're always dependent on someone or something else. (1, 12)

_____ I think I can only charge what the market will bear. And I often underestimate what the market will bear. (6, 7, 8)

(Continued)

What Blocks Me from Making More Money *(Continued)*

_____ I believe no one will pay for what I have or do. (2)

_____ I don't shoot for the limit in terms of money. (7, 9)

_____ I don't duplicate myself, and I can be in only one place at a time. That limits the amount I can make. (6)

_____ I have no idea what making more looks like. I'm too busy to focus on that. (1)

_____ I don't invest at least 10 percent a year. (9)

_____ No matter how much money I make, it's never enough. (1, 9)

_____ I define success by how much money I make. You have to keep score somehow. (1, 9)

_____ I don't see any other ways to make more money. (8)

_____ I've never asked my customers or my employer to help me generate more income. (7)

_____ I'm paid by how many hours I work. (7, 8)

_____ Your reason _____

WORKAHOLISM

There's an important thing I need to address before I give you specific strategies to Work Less, Make More. I know you're getting anxious to start this process, but this is vital to the work you're going to be doing.

Are you a workaholic?

Okay, that's a slap-in-the-face question. But I needed to ask it.

The phrase "I'm working" receives tremendous support in our business world. There's an air of success to working so hard and so long. Yet if you cross the line to being obsessed about work—

about having only one thing in your life that you do well and it's work—the truth is you're working in order to avoid yourself, your feelings, your family, and your life. You've become a workaholic.

Please understand that many people in today's world spend a lot of time working. Not all of them are workaholics. You need to see the difference in order to make sure you haven't crossed the line. I did.

Yes, I became a workaholic during all of those years of working so much. It was easier for me to work than to face the emptiness I felt in my life. It was easier for me to work than to face the fact that my relationships were falling apart. It was easier for me to work than to admit that everything except work was no longer there. See how easy it is to cross the line?

There is a difference between having passion for your work and workaholism. That difference is not so much the hours you spend, but the emotional fulfillment you get during those hours. For a workaholic, working gives you self-worth. If you're a workaholic, you feel safest when you're working. It's when you feel like you shine, when you communicate best, and when you feel most comfortable. You often put off the rest of your life to work even more.

Part of being a workaholic is also being a victim. When you fall into workaholism, you lose control of your life. You feel trapped by your responsibilities and believe you have no choice but to work longer and harder. You *have* to work late. You *have* to take on more work. You *have* to make the deadline. You *have* to postpone your vacation for a client. The have-to's go on and on.

I saw workaholism in Bob, an old client of mine. The first challenge Bob had was he didn't think he was a workaholic. When I asked him why he worked seven days a week, at least eight hours a day, he simply said, "I have to."

He couldn't understand why his family was bickering about his work. "I support them with the money I make," he said. "I have to work long and hard. If I don't, they won't have the money to do what they want to do. And then they'll be extremely unhappy."

Bob tied up his whole identity into work. He believed he was a good father because he worked to support his family. He believed he was a supportive spouse because he made a lot of money. He believed he was a valuable person because he was a success at work. What he forgot about—and chose to ignore—was being a success in life. We didn't work together for very long because Bob was unwilling to move from being a victim of his work to controlling his life.

Choice is the key word here. If you freely and joyfully work because you're passionate about what you're doing *without* neglecting your relationships, it's not workaholism. The difference between workaholism and overworking is crucial. Workaholism is an addiction that you use to isolate yourself. It's a way to avoid living your life.

Overworking, on the other hand, is a classic problem for many people. As you become more successful, you constantly fight the tendency to bring work home. You're often so tired, the work sits in the corner. You're full of guilt the next morning because you didn't work, and by the time you get to the office, you're cranky. Burned out. Stressed out. In the short term, you get tremendous rewards and recognition from achieving so much. In the long run, you burn out. This book is exactly what you need if you find yourself overworking—a lot.

Remember the difference: If you're a workaholic, you use work to avoid everything else in your life. If you're overworked, you have other interests and important relationships in your life; you just don't spend enough time focused on them.

If you're feeling as if there's a lot of truth in what I'm saying about workaholism, you probably have an issue with it. But don't just take my word for it. Sit down with a professional who's trained to help you get out of the workaholism trap. There are trained therapists who can help you undo the workaholism lifestyle or you can join Workaholics Anonymous. Support groups can be found in most cities.

Please do not be like a friend of mine who one day asked me, "Do you think I'm successful?" I of course said I did. He is a very financially successful man. But that's about it. The work and the money is there; the rest of his life isn't.

He said, "I agree with everything you wrote about being a workaholic, but I'm not one. I just disproved your theory." He instead proved my point. He just wasn't able to see it.

NOW WHAT?

Go back and take a close look at the blocks outlined in this chapter. What are the top five main things that hold you back from working less and making more? Write them down here.

1.

2.

3.

4.

5.

The best way to proceed is to look at the five things that are big thorns in your side and take care of them first. It's often better to go after the behaviors that cause the most problems. You'll feel the biggest relief when you handle these issues, and you'll free up time and space to start making other changes.

But before you start making substantial changes in how you work—and how you live—there's a big thing that still stands in your way. You probably don't know what Work Less, Make More *really* means.

Let's move on to defining it.

DEFINE YOUR VISION

I just got off the phone with a woman who was calling to hire a coach. She told me she was overworked and miserable in her job. She didn't make enough money and didn't have enough time to do what she loved to do; yet everyone around her told her she was successful. She just didn't feel that way, and she had heard I might have the magic pill.

When I asked her what she wanted for her life, all I got was silence. She had no idea. None whatsoever. The "magic pill" theory doesn't work if you don't know what you want your life to be.

She's not the only one. Most people I talk with don't have an idea of what they want their lives to be. They may have fantasies, but when it comes right down to it, I ask them what they really want, and all I get is silence.

Setting a course to Work Less, Make More is like commanding a ship. (That ship happens to be your life.) Your ship may be the newest and shiniest in the fleet, but if it has a faulty compass, it'll take a sheer miracle to get you to your destination. You must have a vision for your work—and more importantly, your life.

What does Work Less, Make More mean to you? That's what I'm talking about when I use the word *vision*. Decide where you want to go on with your life. Otherwise, I promise you, you won't make it.

Having a vision is vital because it'll guide you when the going gets tough. When you're screaming out because you're breaking down the walls of your comfort zone, your vision will inspire you to keep doing what needs to be done. You have to decide what you want if you ever expect to get there.

YOUR VISION

Often when I ask people to define what working less and making more means to them, I get very general statements. Things like:

- I'll feel less stress.
- I won't fight with my spouse about money anymore.
- I'll have time to do what I want.
- I'll feel at peace.
- I'll be able to travel more.

They all sound great in theory, but the problem with these answers is they are not specific. You can't measure these responses. How will you know when you feel less stress? You'll just feel better, right? That just doesn't work as an ultimate destination. At any time, you could feel a bit of stress, and you're suddenly not working less and making more *by your own definition*.

Work Less, Make More can be measured. I want you to see evidence and results from your work in this book. You need to be able to clearly see that your life has changed. You need to know when you are working less and making more. These general "I'll feel better" statements are not specific enough.

Before we go any further to defining your vision, I need to explain the difference between a vision and a goal, because I know some of you think I'm taking you through a goal-setting exercise. A *vision* is a mental picture of what you want your life to be, in this case, in relation to Work Less, Make More. A *goal*, on the other hand, is how you're going to get there. What you're going to do and how you'll measure your results along the way.

For example, perhaps your vision is to make $100,000 a year by working just four days a week. Your goal for the next 90 days is to make 10 calls a day to get referrals from your current customers in order to generate the $100,000. You'll reach your goal when you hit 900 calls in three months. Your vision stays the same, but your goals change along the way. (Of course, you'll create a bigger vision for your life as you continue to expand and grow. . . .)

Get out your pen and ask yourself the questions on the following page to help you define what Work Less, Make More means to you. What does your ideal life look like? Be honest. And don't pay attention to the negative thoughts that pop up. Things like, "Don't be stupid. You could never do that." or "That's a dumb idea. You're not smart enough to accomplish that." Just let those thoughts come and go, and instead focus on what you want your ideal life to look like.

You've started the process of uncovering some key elements to your Work Less, Make More vision. It's time to pull it together to create a vision *for you*. Your vision will excite you when you write

Discover Your Work Less, Make More Vision

1. How many hours do you want to work each day?
2. How many hours do you want to work each week?
3. How many free days do you want to take each week?
4. How many vacations do you want to take each year?
5. What will you do with your free time? Be specific.
6. What type of work brings you joy?
7. What do you need in your work in order to do your best? In other words, describe the ideal environment, people, and resources you need to do your best work.
8. How much money do you need to survive each month?
9. How much more money do you need on top of your basic expenses to feel as if you have enough? Is there a certain amount of money you want in the bank to feel rich? Why that number?
10. How much money do you want to make each month?
11. How much money do you want to make each year?
12. What will you do with this money? Be specific.
13. What's different about your life when you're working less and making more than how you live your life today?
14. What does it look like when you're working less?
15. What does it look like when you're making more?
16. How does it feel when you're working less?
17. How does it feel when you're making more?
18. How will you know when you're working less and making more? What evidence and results will prove it?
19. In what areas in your life do you want to be wealthy? Why?

it down, and it will pull you forward. Make you want to do whatever it takes to get there. If it's the right vision, it'll stir the passion in your soul. Spend some time deciding where it is you want to be. If you don't know where you're headed, like the saying goes, you won't get there.

Here are a few examples of visions my clients have developed. Notice how specific and measurable they are. These clients knew—or will know—exactly when they get there.

- Working less and making more means I'm earning $100,000 per year and working 40 hours a week.
- Working less and making more means work becomes play and my income increases by 10 percent each year.
- Working less and making more means I never have stress headaches, and I earn $250,000 per year doing what I love: selling.
- Working less and making more means I have a staff I can trust completely. I earn $1 million per year while still taking eight vacations a year.
- Working less and making more means I never miss my children's events, and my income goes up by 15 percent each year.
- Working less and making more means my wife doesn't have to work anymore, and I work 40 hours a week.

It's your turn. The key is to develop a compelling vision that is less than 20 words. By limiting the amount of words you use, you won't get caught up in using flowery, unnecessary words that mean nothing. All you have to do is complete the following phrase.

Work Less, Make More means . . .

Can you measure it when you get there? Go back and put a deadline on your vision. For example, *Working less and making* *more means I'll work 40 hours a week doing what I love and make $250 per hour by December 31, 2000.*

How can you make your vision tighter and more concrete? Go back and do it.

OVERCOMING NEGATIVE BELIEFS

Now go back and reread your vision. Spend a few minutes thinking about it. Really imagining it's going to come true.

I know, you have probably already experienced the Critic showing up. The Critic is full of negative, there's-no-way-in-hell-you'll-ever-do-that comments. We all have a Critic, that horrible, negative voice inside our heads that never supports us. It's your Critic's job to sabotage your dreams. It's your Critic's job to point out the reasons why you can't do it. It's your Critic's main purpose to keep you stuck.

This negative voice in your head is not your voice. Did you get that? That critical, judgmental voice is a combination of all the naysayers in your life. It's your mother, father, grandparents, teachers, siblings, friends all rolled into one. Anyone who ever spit on your dreams is now part of the Critic's voice.

The problem is many of you believe what the Critic says. And whatever you believe to be true is true. In order to make your vision a reality, you must change what you believe to be true.

Your beliefs—or the assumptions you hold—direct the course of your life whether you're conscious of them or not. If you believe people are generally good, every experience you have will be shaped by that belief. When someone cuts you off in traffic in the morning, your beliefs about people will tell you that person is inherently good and must be having a bad day. If you believe people are out to get you, you'll react quite differently to the same situation. You may even give the driver an obscene gesture. Your beliefs, both negative and positive, drive your behavior without your even consciously thinking about it.

The same is true about whether you believe you can Work Less, Make More. Your underlying assumptions about a lot of issues—success, money, work, your own abilities—shape whether you'll have success in this program.

One of the first men I coached stopped the process when he was right at the threshold of success. Jake is a top-producing insurance salesperson, and he was tremendously excited when he first learned about Work Less, Make More. He rushed out, bought a journal, and dove head first into redesigning how he worked and lived. As his coach, I was ecstatic with his immediate successes. Things that took other people six months to accomplish— like increasing his income while working five hours less every week—he achieved in a few short weeks.

After about 90 days, we were talking one day, and I noticed his energy was off. Jake sounded depressed. He shared with me that he didn't think it was possible to work less and make more. He had grown up believing that success meant you had to work extremely hard. He believed he had to sacrifice and wait until he someday made it. Jake shared with me that his father had always told him he was lazy. "Son, successful people are always working to get it done right. Stop daydreaming, and start working." Every time he took a day off, Jake would hear his father's voice. He believed what his father believed: Success only comes to those who suffer and sacrifice.

Jake soon told me this program was too easy, and he wasn't going to continue. He went back to a life of working 80 hours a week. Jake's underlying assumption that success equals money was accomplished by the belief that success came only if you personally sacrificed something to get there. For Jake, the sacrifice was his relationship with anyone he didn't work with. Working less and making more enabled him to get back in touch with old friends and with himself, and he felt as if he wasn't focusing enough on being successful.

Jake didn't take the time to change his beliefs about what success means to him. He instead lived his life based on what his father had believed, and that belief soon became his own. He didn't explore his hidden assumption that being rich was evil, and he didn't look at his low self-esteem that said success was reserved for other people. He let his Critic direct the course of his life.

As his coach, I learned an important lesson. It's vital to look at what beliefs shape our lives. Unless you change your beliefs, you'll run back to the way things used to be. You'll make decisions unconsciously and head off in the wrong direction. You may end up like Jake, in the rat race with no way to get out.

Do you believe you can Work Less, Make More? If you believe you can, are you willing to do what it takes to get there?

Working less and making more is not just a 10-point plan that you follow for a few weeks. It's about changing the way you work and live. Many times, it's a massive change. Other times, it's a little tweak to what you're already doing. Work Less, Make More is about changing your life. The only way you can change at the core of your being is to change what you believe.

YOUR BELIEFS ABOUT SUCCESS

The first beliefs you need to look at are your beliefs about success. Changing your perceptions about what it takes to be successful is vital to learning how to work less and make more. Take the Success Rules Quiz on the following pages to test your beliefs.

What do your beliefs about success tell you about how you're living your life? If you believe you have to suffer and sacrifice to be successful, you will resist the direction I give you to live a lifestyle without all the pain and suffering. Your mind will tell you that just doesn't fit with what it takes to be successful. Or you'll stop yourself midstream because something doesn't feel right.

Take out your journal and ask yourself these questions.

1. When you took this quiz, what did you discover about your beliefs about success? What do you believe it takes to be successful?
2. Who told you that you needed to believe this? What exactly did they say? *Don't say no one told you. You got the message from somewhere. Your parents? Coworkers? Mentors? The media? From whom?*

The Success Rules Quiz

Circle **Y** for yes or **N** for no.

Do you feel bad if you don't work at least 10 hours a day?
Y   N

Do you expect to come home tired from work?
Y   N

Do you act as if your company (the one you own or the one you work for) expects you to put its needs first, your family and your own needs last?
Y   N

Do you feel guilty if you say no at work?
Y   N

Do you find yourself taking on more and more work because there's no one else to do it?
Y   N

Is one of your biggest complaints that others don't work as hard as you do? Are you secretly proud of this?
Y   N

Do you measure your success by what you achieve through your work, like financial gains and security?
Y   N

Do you keep going and going even when you want to quit?
Y   N

Do you find yourself cutting your vacations short so you can go to the office?
Y   N

(Continued)

The Success Rules Quiz *(Continued)*

Are you frustrated because the results aren't showing up fast enough?
Y   N

Do you typically spend more than 10 minutes on a problem without asking for help?
Y   N

Are you finding yourself justifying and rationalizing why things are taking so long? You know, excuses like *I don't have enough time. It's sitting on someone's desk. I'm waiting for a call back.*
Y   N

Do you carry your briefcase with you and check your voice-mail and e-mail when you're on vacation?
Y   N

If you said yes to at least three of these, your beliefs about work are limiting your success and ultimately your lifestyle.

---

3. Why do you believe it now? What evidence have you seen in your life to prove to you that this belief is true?
4. How does it serve you to keep believing this? What's the benefit you get from continuing to believe this?
5. Give some examples of how this belief dictates your behavior.
6. What price do you pay by continuing to believe this?
7. How does believing this prevent you from working less and making more?

Your beliefs about success usually come from other people. You look around and see your friends, mentors, and parents working long hours and driving themselves to achieve. You read books that say success is about motivating and pushing yourself to do the things you don't want to do, in order to get the results you think you want. That's what people told me when I was starting my career. I thought in order to be successful I had to work 80 hours a week to prove I was worthy of success.

In fact, one of my favorite bosses early in my career gave me a piece of advice I've never forgotten. He said, "Jen, you need to figure out what you want. Then do anything, and I mean anything, to get there. You'll work long, hard hours. When your friends are out at the bar, you'll be at the office working. Stay committed and focused and someday if you work hard enough, success will be yours." And this was from a guy who I considered to be wildly successful—even though he had an ulcer and had just recently been separated from his wife.

That's my point. These old beliefs about success do work, but you pay a very big price for that success. Work Less, Make More is not about suffering. It's not about sacrifice. *It's about finding a new way of having it all.* Until you change your beliefs about success, the success I'm writing about will elude you.

The trick to integrating these ideas and concepts into your life is first changing how you think and feel. You must shift internally before your external world changes.

YOUR BELIEFS ABOUT MONEY

There are other beliefs that get in the way of working less and making more. They are your beliefs about money.

Often, your beliefs about money are deep seated. In our society, we typically don't openly talk about money. In fact, I've been accused of being only concerned with money just because I ask the question: How much money do you want to make? Money is part of the equation. It's not the final destination, but it is a part of our lives. Ignoring how much you make or don't make is certainly not the answer.

The reason you decided to read this book—you're into it by now—is because there's a part of you who wants more freedom,

Shifts You Need to Make

Old Belief	*New Belief*
I work extremely hard to be a success.	I work extremely smart, not hard.
I work all the time in order to someday "make it."	I stopped working a long time ago. My work is fun and full of joy.
I come home exhausted from work.	I come home from work energized.
I put the company needs in front of my own needs.	I come first. No matter what. Only then can I be brilliant at work.
I take on more and more at work because no one else will do it.	I only take on activities I do extremely well.
I define my success by the money I make.	I define success first by how fulfilled I am. The money comes second or third or fourth.
I cut my vacations short so I can work. Or I don't vacation at all.	I take all the time I need to rest. That way I go back to work on fire.
I keep going and going.	I listen to myself and rest when I need to.
I never ask for help.	I always ask for help. I'm not weak if I ask for help.
I feel guilty because I'm playing but everyone else is working.	I know that I'm on the right path. I don't care what others think.
I live my life by someone else's rules and standards.	I live my life by my own rules and standards.

Adapted from material from Coach University, www.coachu.com. Used with permission.

more independence, and more security. Unless you look at your beliefs about money, unless you find out what assumptions you have about money, you will not gain the freedom you desperately want. No matter how brilliant this program is, your beliefs about money will dictate whether you have money at all.

How do you unearth your beliefs about money? The challenge you'll face in discovering your true feelings is that you often intellectually know one thing about money, but your heart tells you something different. If you take too much time to think about the truth, you simply won't find what beliefs are holding you back.

I have a client who has deep spiritual beliefs. Beth meditates every morning, and she tells me all the time that she trusts she's in the right place at the right time. On many occasions, Beth has a sense of peace about her. A peace that tells the world that she is in the right place doing what she wants to do.

When I asked Beth if she wants to be rich, tremendously wealthy someday, she instinctively gave a resounding yes. Her spiritual beliefs tell her that having money is a good thing, and anyone who wants money can manifest it. My very next question was, "So why aren't you financially wealthy right now?" We both saw a negative belief rearing its ugly head.

Intellectually, Beth believes money will come to her whenever she needs it, but her heart tells her she won't get what she wants. She doesn't completely trust that if she does what she loves— massage therapy—the money will follow. Her head tells her one thing, and her heart tells her something else. Be very interested in what your heart says because that's what your true beliefs are.

As I've worked with many clients around their beliefs about money, I've discovered two main beliefs showing up. The first is that they don't believe they deserve more money, and the second is that they believe they can only be successful if they have lots of money.

Both of these beliefs come from not believing that who they are is enough. Go back to the example I used about Beth. She believed that who she is was not enough to attract more money in her life. Her negative beliefs about herself and her abilities often held her back. That is, until she changed them.

The same thing is true for Richard, another client. He believed that money is the true symbol of success. Without money, he told me, he couldn't be successful. Richard is a top-producing financial planner who has a personality that everyone loves. He's energetic, passionate, focused, and determined. Every year, he competes with himself to keep surpassing his income from the year before. For the past five years in a row, he's beaten his previous personal best.

Richard hired me to help him get a life. He was feeling a lot of stress in keeping up with his lifestyle. He was never able to rest because he was always trying to prove to himself that he's better than he was the year before. He lives in a luxurious home, drives an expensive car, wears the most exquisite clothes. He sends his kids to the most prestigious schools, and his clients are used to the fancy dinners and the elaborate gifts.

When I first starting coaching him, Richard told me he had to compete with everyone else in his industry, and he believed the way to compete was to show everyone else he had the best of everything.

After we had been working together a few weeks, I asked Richard what he found passionate about his work. His answer? The money. When he got right down to it, he was tired of working 80 hours a week in financial planning. He confessed to me that he didn't even like the financial planning industry, but he was making so much money he couldn't imagine doing something different.

I asked him what would happen if he didn't drive his Lexus and work in the most expensive office space in town. He told me, "Jen, I would be a failure. Money is how I measure my success in life. It doesn't matter how happy I am; what matters is how much money I have."

Notice what's going on here. Richard had tightly tied his identity to how much money he makes. Somewhere along the way, he decided to believe that money was the key to happiness, and he focused his whole life toward the accumulation of money. Money became more important than his own happiness. When we got right down to it, Richard was using money to make himself feel important. He believed in his heart that who he is was not good enough, and he was out to prove through money that he did matter.

I believe anyone can have as much money as he or she wants while living a life that nourishes the self. Life is not about sacrificing who you are for some large paycheck. At the end of your life, you won't remember how much money you made. You'll remember the lives that were intertwined with yours.

Does that mean that you should settle for being poor? No, of course not. What it does mean is you stop chasing the money in order to make yourself feel important. It means you live your life by new standards.

In your heart what do you believe about money? Julia Cameron in her book, *The Artist's Way* (G.P. Putnam's Sons, New York, 1992), found a great way to help you uncover the truth. I've used a few of her ideas, and I've added my own. Take the quiz on the following page to test your money beliefs.

Now go back to your answers to that quiz. Open up your journal and answer these questions.

1. When you took this quiz, what did you discover about your beliefs about money? What do you believe it takes to be rich?

2. Who told you that you needed to believe this? What exactly did they say? *Don't say no one told you. You got the message from somewhere. Your parents? Coworkers? Mentors? The media? From whom?*

3. Why do you believe it now? What evidence have you seen in your life to prove to you that this belief is true?

4. How does it serve you to keep believing this? What's the benefit you get from continuing to believe this?

5. Give some examples of how this belief dictates your behavior with money.

6. What price do you pay by continuing to believe this?

7. How does believing this prevent you from working less and making more?

What Does Money Mean to You?

Complete the following phrases quickly and without thinking. Don't censor anything you think or anything you write down. Write whatever comes to your mind first.

1. Rich people are

2. Money makes me

3. I'd have more money if

4. My father thought money was

5. In my family, money caused

6. Money equals

7. My mother thought money would

8. Poor people are

9. If I could afford it, I'd

10. I'm afraid that if I didn't have money, I would

11. Money is

12. Money creates

13. Having money is not

14. In order to have more money, I'd need to

15. When I have money, I usually

16. I think money

17. If I weren't so cheap, I'd

18. My friends think money

19. Being broke tells me

20. Being rich tells me

Shifts You Need to Make

Old Belief	New Belief
I'm not successful if I don't make a lot of money.	Money is just one way to measure success.
I have to work a lot in order to make lots of money.	Investing tremendous amounts of time is not the answer. Value is.
I need to chase money and make it happen.	I push money away when I chase it. I instead let money come to me.
I'll never be rich.	I am wealthy.
Money is a big deal.	Money is a tool in life.
If I have money, someone else won't.	If I have money, others can, too.
I won't make more money than my parents.	I can have as much money as I want.
I cannot live a spiritual life if I have lots of money.	Money is money.
I must work long and hard in order to make it financially.	Making money is part of the plan. Suffering is *optional.*

Adapted from material from Coach University, www.coachu.com. Used with permission.

A big part of learning how to make more is shifting what you believe about money. Just as we looked at success, it's time to look at what used to work and what works today.

My clients find it extremely helpful to shift their definitions of the word *wealth*. What did you just think when you read that word? Most people believe being wealthy has to do with having lots of money. I believe being wealthy is having an abundance in my life. It means having a wealth of money, a wealth of relationships, a wealth of opportunities, a wealth of happiness, a wealth of creativity, a wealth of friendships, a wealth of space and time, and a wealth of love in my life. Success to me means being wealthy in every area of my life. Making more, therefore, means being wealthy.

Richard, the client I told you about a few pages back, has adjusted his definition of success since we've been working together. Success no longer means just money to him. For Richard, success must include wealth in all areas of his life. He has focused his attention on restructuring his financial planning business to get more personal satisfaction from the work he does, and he's been following the Work Less, Make More program to find more abundance in every part of his life. Guess what? It's working. I've never seen him so full of joy and satisfaction. And his income doubled last year when he was focused on making more of his life, not on making more money.

Do your beliefs about money support that quest?

A FINAL THOUGHT

Go back to the Work Less, Make More vision you created earlier in this chapter. Take what you wrote and put it on a sign you can hang all over your home and office. Put the vision on a sign on the bathroom mirror so you see it every time you brush your teeth. Put your vision in your day planner—or in your Palm Pilot—that you carry around with you. Use calligraphy to make the vision a work of art and hang it in your office. Break out your paints and watercolor a cool print. Type it into the computer and print out 10 copies to put everywhere you go in your home. Make your vision larger than life—maybe the size of a poster—so it's constantly in your face reminding you where you're going.

Express your passion about your vision. You will Work Less, Make More. And starting with a vision will help you make that happen.

Exercises

1. Get out your journal. Write about what blocks you from Work Less, Make More. How does it feel to have identified what gets in your way? What can you do to overcome these blocks? Are you willing to do it?

2. Start a list in your journal titled "The 100 things I want to accomplish in the next six months." The trick to doing this type of list is to write down anything that comes to mind. Anything. You can repeat yourself. If you already wrote it down but it's still in your mind, write it down again and again. Just keep writing until you reach 100.

3. Go back to your list of 100. What are the top 10 things you most want to accomplish? Use that list when you're working through this program.

4. Write at the top of a page in your journal, "My payoff for not working less and making more is . . ." Explore what that means to you. Make sure you reflect on the price you're paying by staying where you are.

5. Go back to your past and remember three people who tried their best to squash your dreams. Did they succeed in bringing you down? Write about your experience in your journal.

6. Go back to your past and remember three people who supported you and your dreams. How did it feel to have someone support who you are? Write about your experiences in your journal. Then write them a letter thanking them for their support. You decide whether or not you want to mail it.

7. Take yourself for a 20-minute walk. Alone. A brisk walk can clear the mind like nothing else. You'll want a clear head as you start the Work Less, Make More process. So get moving.

CHAPTER 2

Do What You Do Best

Do not focus on what you love.

Yes, I did write that. So many people I know spend all their time and energy trying to find the one thing they love in order to design their work around it. They believe that if they could only find what they love, the money would follow.

Every time I hear that, I want to scream. Stop wasting your energy. It won't work.

Here's an example to show you why it won't work. Before he started working with me, a client of mine fell into this trap. Matt spent a lot of time—and a lot of money taking career assessments—to figure out what he truly loved. He knew that had to be both something he loved and one that he could earn a living doing.

One day when he was on the golf course, he realized that what he loved was golf. Matt loved the game of golf. He loved holding a golf club in his hand and going for an impossible shot. He loved hanging out with his buddies talking about business, family, life, and golf. Matt loved the smell of freshly cut grass and the way his golf shoes sounded as he walked on cement.

So in following this idea of doing what he loved, Matt spent six months investigating the perfect business that was geared around golf. He soon opened an exclusive retail store specializing in golf equipment. Now please understand that Matt is not someone to take things lightly. He went all out with this store. He had the best lighting, the best location, the best employees, the best inventory, and his clients loved his store. He turned a profit in his first six months, a rare thing in retail. Yet five years later, frustrated, he called me.

He had taken what he loved and had designed a business around it, and what he had found was he hated the retail business. What he loved was golf and he thought owning a business focused on golf would keep him passionate. Matt was lulled into believing if his business had something to do with what he loved, it would all work out. It didn't.

Instead, what I want you to do is focus on what you do best. When you focus on your natural gifts—what I call your brilliance—you will get paid what you want to get paid, you'll work the hours you want to work, and you'll find the satisfaction and fulfillment you've been seeking. The love always comes when you do what you do best. Always.

Work Less, Make More has *nothing* to do with looking at your weaknesses, and it has nothing to do with balancing out your skills. It has to do with focusing on what's brilliant about you. What you shine at doing.

When you're the best at what you do, you decide how much you're going to work and how much you'll get paid. But you can't be the best if all you're focused on is doing what you love. Be smart about designing your life around your strengths. They are the secret weapons you need to Work Less, Make More.

Just look at Michael Jordan. He got paid millions of dollars a year because he became a master at the game of basketball. He honed his strengths and became even better at what he already did well. And he was paid handsomely for it *every* day. Yet when Jordan spent time focusing on baseball, he wasn't tuning into his brilliance. Sure, he was having fun, but he wasn't maximizing his strengths and talents. He was the best at basketball, and he found the love of the game while he focused on being the best.

Today when he's in front of a camera for numerous TV commercials, he's using other gifts he has. You aren't limited to just one gift. You are brilliant at many different things.

If you're thinking, "But Jen, that's Michael Jordan. He's more talented than I am," take a look at a client of mine.

Dennis is a perfect example of how your brilliance can maximize your life. Dennis spent most of his career working his way up the corporate ladder. His last three or four jobs were in high-level executive positions with Fortune 500 companies. He often laughs and says, "I'm not quite sure how I got those jobs, but somehow I did." Dennis was the type of guy people would look at and say, "Wow. That Dennis is so successful." His brilliance is his ability to connect with all sorts of people. He loves to tell stories and make people laugh.

Denny's last few years working in corporate America were extremely difficult. When he drove to the office in the morning, his stomach would be tied up in knots. He hated his job. He despised his boss, and he knew he couldn't go one more day working there. Yet every morning he got into his car and did it again. He was "successful," so how could he quit? Dennis was so busy trying to survive, a part of his soul died.

One day, he had a breaking point. He left his secure, prestigious job, and he moved back to his hometown to become an entrepreneur. Dennis wanted the taste of freedom he thought entrepreneurship would bring. He wanted to run his own show and live his life the way he wanted to live. So he opened his own coffee shop.

When Dennis and I first started to work together, he had been in business about a year. He was working 12 hours a day at the cafe, yet he still managed to spend little time with his customers. He thought that was what his employees were for and used his time to do paperwork or run errands. Dennis was also a smoker, and, smoking like a chimney, he spent most of his time buried in his 10 × 10 office doing the stuff he thought he needed to do to run his business. What else do you do if you're a smoker holed away in a small office every day?

As we worked together, I helped Dennis realize that his real strength was connecting with people, so we decided to shift his schedule to spend more time with his customers. Yes, doing what he did best, which was connecting with other people.

Dennis would spend two hours a day connecting with his customers, telling them stories, finding out about their lives, laughing at funny cartoons. Soon his creativity exploded, and he started developing innovative programs to bring in more customers.

Dennis started to realize that his customers were becoming his extended family, and he noticed that whenever you walk into someone's home, you always notice the pictures of the family members all around. Dennis wanted to do the same thing with his extended family. He started taking photos of his regular customers, and he framed their photos and put them on a wall in his coffee cafe called the Latte Wall Of Fame.

Now if you're a regular customer at his cafe, you will go back to the office and tell all your coworkers about this crazy coffee shop owner who took your picture and put it on the wall. Your coworkers would *have* to go to the cafe to see your mug shot and make fun of you. Soon, your family and friends would be doing the same thing.

Dennis's place was swarming with business all because *he focused on what he did best.*

Simultaneously, Dennis started an exercise program, quit smoking, and cut back his work hours without its hurting his bottom line. He honed what he did extremely well rather than doing the things he thought he should do as a business owner.

Does Dennis struggle with designing his business around his brilliance? Of course he does. There are times when he struggles with finding the time to spend with his customers. Equipment breaks, employees quit, family challenges come up. Yet Dennis knows the key to his success is connecting with people. He keeps that idea top of mind and creates a way to do what he does best.

DISCOVER YOUR BRILLIANCE

The biggest problem with designing your life around what you do best is discovering what that is. Frank Broyles, a University of Arkansas football coach, once said: "Our strength is that we don't have any weaknesses. Our weakness is that we don't have any real strengths."

Think about that. Your weakness is that you don't have any real strengths. Many of you have spent your whole career trying to balance your strengths and weaknesses. Why? Because you've been trained to focus on your weaknesses. When you sat down for a performance evaluation sometime in your life—maybe many times in your life—your manager probably spent the first 15 minutes telling you what you did well during the past year. But the next 45 minutes were spent focused on what you need to improve on.

If you're anything like I was, you'd spend the whole year focusing your time, attention, and passion on improving your weak areas. You were determined to get a much better evaluation the next year. And most of you were successful. You accomplished what you set out to do, and you improved in your weaker areas. What happened to your strengths? They stayed the same.

What you got was balance, and what you also got was boring. You looked at your brilliance, took it for granted, and it became dull and unused. Sure, you improved your weaknesses. But your strengths stayed the same. In today's marketplace, that's the kiss of death.

Why? Because you ended up with skills like everyone else. You cannot leverage your strengths in the market if you're just like everyone else. My marketing consultant Vickie Sullivan says it best: "Whatever is abundant becomes diluted. Whatever is diluted becomes a commodity." Yes, your skills have become a commodity. There's no way you can work less and make more if your skills are a commodity. That's the exact opposite of how to make this happen.

What in your life are you brilliant at? In your heart, you know what you do best. It may be your sharp mind. Your leadership in difficult situations. Your ability to sell anything to anyone. Your brilliance is what you're good at, that also energizes and inspires you as you use it. You often can't see your brilliance clearly because you're naturally good at it. It's right under your nose, and we all know you can't see what's right under your nose.

Let's spend some time uncovering what you do best. Take out a pen and your journal and answer these questions. You may want to take some time to get in a quiet place so you can really concentrate.

1. What do you do easily and naturally?
2. What do your customers pay you for?
3. What does your company pay you for?
4. What have other people said you're really good at?
5. What activities energize you?
6. What consumes you? You know, the stuff that lights your fire.
7. What do you really want to do on your days off?
8. What qualities and skills do you see in other people that you know you have?

Often, many people have a hard time identifying what they do well. Our society has spent a lot of time and energy teaching you how to identify your weaknesses. You simply don't take enough time to focus on your strengths. Sometimes you need some help seeing your true gifts.

Your assignment: Ask five people whom you trust what they see as the gifts you have. Be sure they understand that you expect their brutal honesty. What do they see in you that you can't see?

If you still can't get a grip on what you do well, take the time to hire a professionally trained success coach. Your coach will be able to help you identify your brilliance and give you guidance on how to redesign your life around your strengths. This can be a tough thing to flush out, so please get help if you need it. It's important.

Once you've finished exploring your strengths, complete the following statement:

I am brilliant at . . .

BECOMING A MASTER

Now that you've identified your brilliance, it's time to move you to the next level. Let's go back to the Michael Jordan example I use earlier. Jordan has a great gift for the game of basketball. Yet he didn't rely just on his natural talent. Jordan became a *master* at basketball. Yes, a master. Someone who knows the game backward and forward. The one who is constantly trying new stuff, experimenting with new techniques and strategies. The one who focused on his gifts and worked on making them even stronger. His mastery was rewarded with an enormous salary, raving fans, and the ability to do what he loves every day.

Jordan did the same thing with his gift for performing. He became a master entertainer. A grand performer. That's why he's paid millions of dollars for commercial endorsements every year.

Our society pays extremely well for mastery. Who is the best pro golfer? No matter who you identified, I bet he is paid extremely well. What about the best corporate leader? Again, a big income earner. Look at Mother Teresa. If you know anything about her life, you'd know she built a huge pile of money to help her cause. She was a master at caring and connecting on a deep level with people, and money came in from around the world to help her because people were drawn to her mastery. Did you catch that? They were *attracted* to her mastery. That's what I want for you.

Masters have learned the basics of the craft or industry they are in. They understand what it takes to be competent. But they aren't satisfied with being just like everyone else, so they focus on becoming excellent at their craft. They become excellent salespeople or excellent managers or excellent plumbers or excellent mediators. Yet they still have a passion to learn more, so they focus on becoming a master. They notice the subtleties and nuances that other people just don't see. More important, they begin to create and develop new ideas and strategies because they are that good. They come up with things excellent contributors would not have seen or cared about. They are more than experts. They are masters.

Masters understand they still have so much left to learn, yet they are still the best at what they do. To continue to be the best, they keep learning, growing, and expanding.

What do you need to do to become a master in your craft or industry? The real fun in becoming a master is it allows you to start innovating. Creating. Giving yourself the chance to experience new ways of playing your game.

For those of you who love golf, here's a great example. When you first learn to play golf, you practice the fundamentals until you can hit the ball. You make many mistakes when you're first learning, but you want to play the game, so you keep focused on hitting the ball until you can do it consistently well.

You then polish up your basic skills and lower your score by playing *a lot*. You begin to realize that talking about your score and sharing golf stories are quite different from actually playing a round of golf. So you play even more. You learn that each shot has nothing to do with the last, and you start beating the people who used to beat you.

Learning to become a professional golfer is much harder. To go from good to master is tougher than getting from unskilled to good. Each level of advancement takes work. It also takes an unusual amount of dedication and focus to move from a high level of skill to an even higher level. Many people go for mastery and quit before they get there. They simply aren't willing to stay in the game long enough to become a master.

It takes time, patience, and help from other masters to become a

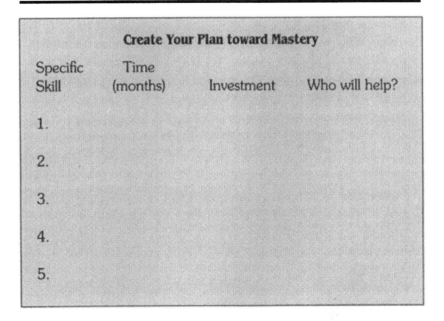

Create Your Plan toward Mastery

Specific Skill	Time (months)	Investment	Who will help?
1.			
2.			
3.			
4.			
5.			

master yourself. You'll need to develop a plan to help you get to that master level. What can you start doing to propel you to that level? On the chart above, identify the five skills that would move you to mastery if you invested the appropriate amount of time and money.

Take the time to build a plan to complete these tasks. Continue to come up with new and better ways of mastering your brilliance. We all want to work with the best—and we'll pay for it. *It's your job to be your best.*

HOW TO PROFIT FROM YOUR BRILLIANCE

One of the most difficult things is to take your brilliance and package it in a way that will earn you money. A vital part of Work Less, Make More is making sure you focus your talents around something that people want to buy. It's important you grow in a way that brings you new profits. Adds more value. Makes you unique in the marketplace. Having talent is not the issue—we all have unique gifts and talents. The key is honing what you do well that people will pay for.

And remember what Vickie Sullivan always says: "What is abundant becomes diluted. Whatever is diluted becomes a commodity." I want you to become a master at what you do well so you're no longer like everyone else. That's what being a master is all about.

A woman I know is great at calligraphy. She was interested in making money at her brilliance, but she couldn't see how to make a good living at calligraphy. It was a side business for her, earning her an extra $200 to $1,000 per month. Certainly not enough money to live on.

I challenged her to come up with ways to profit from her brilliance. Here are some examples of what she came up with:

- Addressing wedding invitations (what she was already doing).
- Specialized corporate work.
- Contracting out to wedding planners and bridal registries.
- Teaching calligraphy classes.

Typical answers, don't you think? Will any of these help her to Work Less, Make More? Probably not, because in each circumstance, she was exchanging time for money. If she doesn't do the work, she won't get paid. I asked her to think bigger. To really expand where she was coming from. To ask herself an important question: What would *a master* in calligraphy get paid for? Look at how the list changed.

- Develop a How to Master Calligraphy book series for those wanting to improve their skills. Sell to thousands of bookstores and art supply houses.
- Write a textbook for teachers of calligraphy on how to speed up the learning curve of students.
- Greatly improve my calligraphy style so I can develop a brand new typeface that can be licensed and sold to thousands of users. My own typeface!

I just love point #3. That's what masters would do—develop their own typefaces. Now that's a big money maker.

Do you see the difference? Packaging your mastery around

what the market will buy is crucial for the Work Less, Make More program. Ask yourself this question over and over again: *What would a master in this area get paid for?*

Keep asking the question until you find the right answer for your own brilliance. Then develop a plan in your journal to get yourself to that level so you can get paid for your mastery.

Discovering your brilliance and designing your life around it is an important part of the Work Less, Make More program. The last thing I want to see you do is focus your life on something that brings you money but doesn't nourish your heart and your spirit. Making more out of your life starts with doing what you do best— all the time.

Exercises

1. Think back to a time in the past 20 years when you were on fire, doing things that you really enjoyed. Describe your experiences in your journal. What were you doing that made the experiences so fulfilling? How can you use that information to make a change in your life?

2. If your brilliance is a style or a quality—like your humor or ability to connect with someone—look at your calendar. What can you do to add your brilliance to everything you do? Go ahead and start doing it.

3. Pretend that you're an explorer. How would another explorer use your brilliance? Write about your experience in your journal. Do the same pretending you're a warrior, an artist, and a judge. What insights are you discovering to help you design your life around what you do best?

4. Brainstorm at least 20 ways you can generate more income based on what you know of your brilliance. How can you make money by focusing on what you do extremely well? Make an action plan for at least one idea. Then do it.

5. Write a letter to yourself daring yourself to design your life around your brilliance. Write with passion and determination that you dare yourself to go out and do it. Dare yourself to overcome the fear of losing it all and instead focus on what you could gain.

6. Who are the people you admire because they are masters at what they do? What qualities and skills do they have? How many of those qualities and skills do you have, too? Which ones can you develop? Spend some time reflecting on who you are and what you need to do to become a master.

7. Develop a plan in your journal to get you from good to mastery. Or maybe from novice to mastery. What guideposts have you set up to help you see your progress? When will you know you arrived? How will you ensure you're enjoying the journey?

CHAPTER 3

Harness the Power of Focus

You have to stop trying to get more done.

I know, you think this chapter is about helping you cram more into your day so you'll get more accomplished. You think that if you would only be more productive, get more done in less time, then you'll finally feel the fulfillment and satisfaction that eludes you.

You're already doing more with less. You've taken the seminars, read the books, learned how to use your planner to prioritize your To Do list. You're actually getting more and more done, but feeling less and less satisfied. Why? Because you've been doing the wrong things.

Harnessing the power of focus comes down to this one idea: Do less to achieve more.

Yes, I'm going to show you how to do less in your day, and get better results. Often what you're doing is jamming more and more into your day, and getting less and less done. You're not focusing your attention on the things that matter the most.

If you want to Work Less, Make More, you must stop focusing on getting more stuff done. You instead must focus on results that matter.

Often people desperately want to follow the 10 steps outlined here, but they're unable to focus enough to get anything done. They're too busy putting out fires rather than planting seeds. This book is about planting seeds. Most of the stuff you do at work is putting out fires.

Instead of scattering yourself by responding to the tidal wave of work that comes at you every day, it's time for you to decide what really counts. Don't hinder your results by trying to do too many things at once. Only by sharply focusing yourself can you achieve the vision you've created.

Let me give you the perfect example of what *not* to do. One of my clients was a typical entrepreneur. By the time she hired me, Sherri had fallen into the trap of juggling too many tasks. Not only was Sherri trying to manage her team of three employees, she was also the bookkeeper, inventory control specialist, marketing manager, production manager, clerical worker, and boss. She spent 80 percent of her time on things that had to get done, yet these activities were clearly not her brilliance. Worse, most of what she spent her time on didn't bring her the results she wanted.

What Sherri did extremely well was find great work by artists and market their products through her catalog. She was inspired to develop new ways to sell their work, yet she was frustrated. She had little time to do what she did best and what mattered the most.

Sherri thought because she was the owner of the company, she *had* to do all the work. What happened was her "responsibilities" took time away from the really important stuff, and her business was suffering even though she was working 60 hours a week or more. Sherri thought trying to get more done would bring her the results she wanted. It didn't. Instead what she got was an anxious feeling because she felt as if she weren't getting anywhere. The truth was, Sherri wasn't getting anywhere.

While Sherri worked with me, she learned how to harness the power of focus. She slowly and cautiously reformatted her business to focus her attention on what she did best and what mattered the most. Sherri was determined to have her business work for her, not against her, so she experimented with a variety of ways to ease her burden. She applied the concepts I had shared with her and dramatically turned her business—and her life—around.

Sherri's creativity blossomed. Fabulous artists started to seek her out. She began an exercise program in order to direct some of her anxiety from her cash flow issues, and it helped tremendously. Sherri also found the right employees to support who she is and what her brilliance is. They took care of the administrative work, and Sherri took care of the big picture, visionary work.

If you're not an entrepreneur, the power of focus also applies if you work for someone else. You are often hired to do one thing—the thing that adds incredible value for the company—but you get caught up in returning phone calls, going to meetings, answering e-mails, going to more meetings. This administrative stuff sucks time away from the most important things. The solution: Focus on results. (A hint: The results that truly matter also reflect your brilliance. Both concepts go hand in hand.)

THE 80/20 RULE

If you look at your own life, if you look closely, you'll soon realize that very little time is spent on what you do *really, really* well. The first lesson in learning how to harness the power of focus is called the Pareto Principle, more commonly known as the 80/20 Rule. Let me show you how this works.

Make a list in your journal of all the tasks you do at work in a typical week. Include everything, even the smallest thing that takes only five minutes. You know, like sending an e-mail, opening the mail, or making a copy. Write it all down. Use another piece of paper if you need to.

Rather than trying to come up with the whole list now and missing something, keep a notebook out where you can see it all week and record the stuff you actually do. It may be a wise idea to record this in a section in your day planner if you carry that around with you all the time.

Record everything that takes more than five minutes. You will often forget the little things that take up your time. Go through your calendar and look at where you've spent your time in the past. Your calendar often gives you a big clue on where you invest your time and energy.

Make a list of at least 50 items where you invest your time. Don't tell me you can't do it. I have clients who end up with 200 or more items on their list. On the page opposite are some examples of items that have shown up on my clients' lists.

What is on your list? Once your list is finished, let's evaluate what's going on.

1. How many hours do you work in a typical week? _____
2. Go back and record next to each item how much time in a typical week that you spend on each activity.
3. Go back to the list and star the three most important activities that you do on a weekly basis. When I say most important, I mean those activities that give you the highest payoff. If you could only do more of them, you'd be adding tremendous value to your career or business. These activities should also be what you're great at doing. Remember, passion + mastery = wealth in every area of your life.
4. Compare how much time you spend on your high-payoff activities versus how much time you spend on all the other stuff.
5. What percentage of your time is spent on nonhigh-payoff activities? Write it down here. _____

Most people find that they spend a maximum of 30 percent on their high-payoff activities. Imagine what would happen to your income if you spent 80 percent of your time on the really important stuff. That's how to use the 80/20 rule to harness the power of focus. Spend 80 percent of your time on the three most important activities that will bring you the greatest results.

Examples of What Takes Up Your Time

1. Listening to voicemail.
2. Reading e-mail.
3. Sending memos.
4. Reading the mail.
5. Weekly/monthly staff meetings.
6. Returning phone calls.
7. Handling customer complaints.
8. Meeting with customers.
9. Meeting with the boss (if you have one).
10. Meeting with suppliers.
11. Conference calls.
12. Surfing the Internet.
13. Handling "emergencies."
14. Interruptions at the office from family.
15. People in the office talking endlessly.
16. More meetings.
17. Training classes that last a whole day.
18. Hanging around the coffee machine.

THE POWER OF THREE

When you read #2 in the exercise opposite, I know what you were thinking: "That's ridiculous. I have more than three things to do!" Before you resist this idea, pay close attention to the Power of Three. Anyone at any time can put only focus and en-

69

ergy behind three things. Three projects. Three big ideas. When you really put your passion behind three things, amazing results show up. Miraculous things. You're building momentum that allows you to get results faster than you do when you're juggling a multitude of things. Momentum is the key here. It's vital to Work Less, Make More.

I first learned about the Power of Three from an innovative entrepreneur in Columbus, Ohio. When Dave was running his company (he's retired now because he learned how to work less and make more!), he demanded that his staff work only on three projects at a time. He told me his team dropped too many balls when they were juggling more than three projects at a time. It was his job to make sure no one dropped anything, so he reduced their chances of doing it. Dave inherently understood the power of focus, and he required his employees to harness the power as well.

The Power of Three is the ultimate in concentration of power. You are more powerful if you're able to concentrate. If you're juggling more than three important projects or priorities, you're bound to forget something. It's usually something important. So you decide you need to start a list of all the stuff you need to remember, and then you lose the list. Or you put the list on a Post-it note, and you just can't seem to find where you put it. When you're focused on three main deliverables, you don't need to do a list.

Okay, let me give you an example of how this works. I have a client who's a residential real estate agent. When we first started working together, Lauren was working seven days a week at least twelve hours a day. She was always feeling frazzled and disorganized because her list was at least 50 items long. All the time.

When I asked Lauren what her three most important things were, the three activities she needed to do to get results that mattered, here's what she told me:

1. Serve current clients.
2. Find new sellers—people who wanted me to sell their properties.
3. Find new buyers—people who want to buy my listings.

But when I looked at Lauren's list, almost 75 percent of the items on the list had nothing to do with these three most important things. We'll talk later about what to do with all these things that "have" to get done, but let's finish working on the Power of Three.

Lauren brought up an excellent point as we were doing this exercise. She said, "Jen, it's easy to identify the three main areas where I need to invest the majority of my time and energy. But under each area, there are at least 50 things to do in each category." Good point.

So we took the Power of Three one step further. What are the three most important things you can do—the three things that would matter the most to your customers when you serve them? Lauren needed to think about this for a while. It was easy for her to get overwhelmed by all the stuff she needed to do, but making a decision on the three things that mattered the most when she was serving a client? That's my point.

Under each area, identify three things that you can do to bring the best results. Good. Now spend 80 percent of your time on these three things.

When you focus on the three most important things, there's little chance you'll forget what you're doing. You free up time and space to develop strong enhancements to your work that you simply would have missed otherwise. If you don't focus, you won't be able to give 100 percent of your effort, and you dramatically reduce your chances for success.

The Power of Three actually frees up time. Instead of stretching you thinner, focus keeps you from overextending yourself. It allows you to give more hours to the few things that matter the most. In an overly complex world, simplicity is the key. The Power of Three also allows you to harness the power of the moment. You'll get more done in less time when you're on a roll.

One of my clients, Jane, is a marketing consultant. She knows that building strong relationships is the key to success in her business, so Jane found herself taking advantage of everything. She joined three networking groups, went to two different chamber functions every week, worked with centers of influence, and joined

10 professional associations. One of her clients asked her to take the lead on a high-profile volunteer project. How could she say no to a client? She didn't.

The next thing she knew, Jane was in charge of fundraising for another nonprofit group. Her phone rang off the hook. Her calendar was jammed, but her income wouldn't grow. In fact, what she most wanted—more business—eluded her.

It's obvious why Jane was not working less and making more. She was spread too thin. Over the course of six months of working with this program, Jane whittled down her networking activities to three high-quality groups. Her business increased by 40 percent. Yes, 40 percent. More importantly, she had time to relax and have more fun in her life. Jane used the power of focus and got the results she wanted. She learned how to work less and make more.

What are the three most important activities you can do? What are the three activities that bring you the greatest return? Write them down here.

1.

2.

3.

Still having trouble choosing three things? I know, most people swear that they can't decide on only three things. Everything you do is important, right? Maybe, but there are three major focuses you need to have in order to harness the power of three. They typically fall into the three categories described in the following sections.

Your Own Purpose for Being

Why are you on this planet? Why is your business in business? Sure, it's to serve customers, but the real reason you're in business is to make a profit and have fun doing it. Are you focusing your attention on these two priorities?

Always focus your attention on your purpose of being so you can make sure your life reflects that. Your business has a purpose of being, too. (Go back to Chapter 2: Do What You Do Best to help you integrate what your business does and what you do well.) In business, we often call this your *market niche*. You can't be all things to all people. Maximize what you do best.

One of my clients, Dan, epitomizes what it means to run his business by his purpose of being. Dan is a tremendously successful health insurance salesperson who many people simply adore. He has a sense of peace about him, and he's always interested in helping someone out. Dan knows he's alive to serve other people, and he does it in his life and in his business.

About two years ago, Dan worked with a marketing consultant to help him identify his most profitable clients. He realized that his ideal customer is a small business owner with a minimum of five employees. Because of the time and energy he puts into every client, he actually loses money if he works with companies with less than five employees on the health plan.

Yet Dan understood that his purpose of being—to serve—does not mean he simply turns business away. Instead, he set up a strategic alliance with another insurance salesperson to handle the small accounts. Now Dan is able to serve his clients without losing money. He harnesses the power of focus tremendously well.

If you would look at Dan's schedule, you would see that how he spends his time is focused on serving other people. His business calendar reflects that and so does his personal calendar. The power of focus is about knowing what you do best and focusing your time and attention there.

Your Current Clients

Successful people know exactly who they're doing work for. Your target markets include current customers and potential customers. If you work within a corporation, who is your target market? Don't say you don't have one because you do. Your boss? Your CEO? Your staff? Your company's customers? If you own your own business, your current customers are not only your paying customers, but also your employees. You need to invest time to maintain great relationships with both your customers and your employees.

How you spend your time needs to be focused on your current customers. To continue to work less and make more, you must develop new programs that add more value to the lives of your customers. How can you help them save time? How can you help them save money?

If all you do is run around reacting to what they say they need, you'll miss the opportunity to expand, learn, and grow. You open yourself up for the possibility someone else will be able to do the job quicker, better, and easier. It's vital that you use the power of focus to zero in on your current customers.

Your Future Customers

When you know what you do and what you stand for, you'll naturally keep an eye out for future opportunities. An important part of staying in the game is watching for new opportunities and taking advantage of them. Are you spending your time exploring your future?

This is one area most people fail to invest much time in. You're so busy rushing around checking things off your To Do list, you fail to invest your energy in what really matters. This world is changing very quickly, and it's important to have the time and space to explore new areas or new opportunities.

Remember my client Sherri that I told you about a few pages back? She's the owner of a company that sells artwork. Sherri was like most other people. She was so busy handling customer orders, employee problems, shipping issues, equipment breakdowns, and other daily crises that she spent very little time focusing on future opportunities. One of her competitors in the Midwest was developing some aggressive customer programs and taking many of her customers away. Sherri was forced to react to this competitor and play his game rather than have the foresight to set the rules of their competition.

If you whittle down 80 percent of your time on these three areas—your purpose of being, your current customers, and your future customers—you'll find you are able to get better results by actually doing less. The Power of Three works.

HOW TO DESIGN YOUR LIFE AROUND THREE

You want to know what to do with all the stuff that doesn't fit into your high-payoff activities. These things have to get done, right? Well, maybe.

One of my associate coaches, Chuck Proudfit, came up with a clever mantra that will help you clean off your plate. It's called Eliminate—Delegate—Automate. Let's look at each one to help you get rid of everything that doesn't fall into your Power of Three.

Eliminate

This is perhaps the easiest one of all. It simply means DON'T DO IT. I believe at least 50 percent of what's on your list doesn't need to get done. You're caught up in justifying your existence by checking more things off your To Do list each day. Dump everything and anything you can. Be brutal with this.

In fact, go back to the list you made a few pages ago and start crossing things off your list. Experiment with not doing something and see if anyone notices. If they don't notice, it wasn't important. This week I want you to dump at least 20 percent of the projects you currently have in your life. It'll help you build momentum to start dumping more and more.

Delegate

When you're focused on working less and making more, take my advice. You must delegate everything but your brilliance. Yes, everything. Rather than forcing yourself to be good at accounting, hire someone to handle your bookkeeping. Not organized? Find someone to keep your life in order. You can always write a check for what you're not good at.

Just the other day, I asked my assistant to reorganize the office. It was her job to go through what had accumulated over the past year and purge the clutter. It was something I wanted to do, but I knew it would have taken me at least two hours to do it. Better to delegate it to her, because she's much better at organizing than I'll ever be.

I was busy at the computer writing my syndicated column, and Pat was hauling full trash bags out of my office. I was focused on revenue-producing activities, and she was focused on doing a necessary task that I would never have gotten done. I can't tell you how wonderful it felt not to be concerned with the details of cleaning out the office. Did she know what should have been tossed out and what didn't? Of course not, but she asked when she needed to.

Some of you are asking yourself this question: "What if Pat had thrown out something that I really needed?" She didn't, but if she had, I believe most things can be replaced. The payoff for having her clean up the mess was much greater than any mistake she would have made. Did you get that? The payoff was greater having someone else do it.

Ask yourself: "Who can help complete this project or task so I can stay focused on my most important activities?" If you don't have anyone to delegate to (a common excuse I often hear), maybe it's time to hire someone.

How do you know when it's the right time to hire someone? First, decide how much money you make an hour when you're focusing on revenue-producing activities. Then evaluate how much time you'd save if you had some assistance. How much more money would you make? In 99 of 100 cases, the additional money earned far outweighs the cost of a new staff person.

The key to delegating is you're giving the responsibility of getting something done to someone besides yourself. Delegation is about ridding yourself of your weaknesses and letting someone else handle them. Here are some important things to keep in mind when you're delegating projects to someone else.

Delegate. Don't Dump

You will not be able to effectively delegate if you push your projects onto someone else. Make sure the other person is motivated to help you with your tasks. More importantly, be sure to take the extra time to discuss everything that needs to get done.

So many times, I see people dump projects into someone's lap, then get angry because the other person screwed them up. That's not the way to delegate. If you're going to delegate, give yourself ample time to train the person to do the tasks the way you like them. You must remember that the person you're delegating to is new at this. No one can read your mind, so if he or she messes up the first few times, take responsibility and realize you did a poor job in training.

One of my clients is a fast-paced entrepreneur who owns a kitchen and bath design company. Troy is the perfect example of someone who dumps projects into his employees' laps. Troy is extremely busy. He not only runs the business, but he sells at least 60 percent of the company's total revenues each year. He's always running out the door while "delegating" a project. He takes less than five minutes to explain his task, and he expects his staff to do it right the first time. That's what I call dumping. Take the time to train your staff so they understand how to complete the projects to your standards.

Delegate Only If You've Developed a Frequent Reporting Process

Often the reason people don't delegate is because they don't trust anyone else to do the task. My clients tell me this all the time: "Jen, I can do it better than they can." You know what? You can do it better than they can right now because you haven't taught them how to do it right. Does that mean you should spend your time doing it? The answer is no. Why would you want to spend your time on a job that's worth $10 an hour rather than focus your attention on tasks that earn you $100 an hour or more? The key is to look at the amount of time you're losing by not focusing on high-payoff activities. You pay a big price when you don't learn to trust someone else.

One of the reasons you don't trust is because you fear the worst. You think if someone else screws up, you're the one who will have to clean up the mess. Catch the mistakes before they happen by instituting a daily reporting system. You'll feel more comfortable because you'll know what's going on, and you won't feel as if you're losing control. It's much less time consuming to oversee a process than do the tasks yourself.

Delegate to the Right Person

A rule of thumb to use is this: After they're trained, people you delegate to must be able to do the task twice as well as you could. Yeah, twice as well. Measure their success by how much value they add to your life. Do they take advantage of opportunities you didn't have time to see? Do they accomplish projects without your asking them to complete them? Are they excited to come up with new and better ways of operating? If they do not meet your standards, find someone who will add real value to your life.

Work Less, Make More is not about lowering your standards. A high priority for you is finding the right people to join your support team. Who is the ideal person you would want to give important assignments to? Describe that person, then go out and find him or her.

Create Partnerships That Focus on Individual Strengths

In some cases, it may be difficult for you to hire someone to handle these important tasks. Why not trade out what you don't want to do?

It's a good idea to develop a partnership and share strengths with each other. One of my clients hated to clean the house, but she loved to garden. Her neighbor hated to do her gardening, but really enjoyed cleaning the house. They created a partnership and swapped services. It worked extremely well. They both did what they liked to do, and the other stuff got done. Who can you swap services with?

Another one of my clients has become a master at bartering. Elaine is the owner of a small magazine, and during her first two years in business, cash flow was tight. Rather than give up her business, Elaine developed powerful relationships with other companies and traded advertising for their services. She worked out partnerships to get cleaning services, a new car, restaurant meals, computers, administrative help. Just about everything she needed someone else to do, she found a way to get those services. You don't need lots of money to delegate your nonimportant tasks. You simply need a dose of creativity.

Automate

In this world of ever-changing technology, it's vital for you to start using automation. Once you've eliminated everything you can, and once you've delegated everything you can, it's time to improve your systems so your computer does the work for you.

Did you know that there are companies who provide web-based outsourcing services? All you do is visit their web site, sign up for their services, and you've automated your processes. You can delegate parts of your work—like running employee benefit statements, handling salary research before a performance review, collecting debts, handling communications with your customers—all with the click of your computer. That's just one example of how to use automation to free up your time.

I won't spend a lot of time telling you how to automate your systems—there are plenty of great books out there that can help you do that—but let me share a few stories that illustrate what I'm talking about. The first has to do with me and money. The second with my client and forgetting.

Before I decided to automate my accounting system (and before my company became too big to do all this by hand), I used to collect receipts in a big box. I had been audited by the IRS before—what business owner hasn't?—and I knew I had to keep a hard copy of everything.

I would throw all the receipts into a big box that I had placed under my desk, and I'd tell myself that someday soon I would get to that task. Organizing the receipt box showed up on my To Do list every single day.

Did I ever get around to the task? No, but I sure used a lot of time and energy beating myself up because I never did. Then February of the next year would come around, and I would have to clear off my calendar *for an entire week* to organize my receipts for my taxes. And every year I would curse myself out for not organizing my receipts in an easier way. I just couldn't imagine sitting down once a month and writing everything into a large ledger.

Then I decided to automate. You probably know there is great accounting software on the market for under $200. I use Quicken. This system does everything. Today my assistant goes through the receipts at the end of each month, enters them in the computer, and all I have to do is examine the results of my month. All because I finally understood what it means to automate.

What about my client and her issue with forgetting? I bet you're probably like Mel, and you have a ton of things going on in your head. Mel is a vice president for a well-respected bank, and one of her main responsibilities is working with new or current customers. She's like most of us when she promises to deliver certain things to her customers at specific times of the month. The problem was Mel loved lists. She always had at least four lists going at a time, and not one of the lists was coordinated with the others. She'll never admit it to anyone else, but Mel told me she was forever missing deadlines for her customers. She simply forgot something was due.

Rather than continue to beat herself up, Mel decided to automate her To Do list. She bought a database software with a calendar and reminder system, and now rather than force herself to remember anything, the computer does it for her. When Mel comes into the office in the morning, she turns on her computer and it tells her what she needs to do that day. She programmed her system so the computer will not allow her to move to another screen until she clicks off that she's completed that task. By 10 A.M. each morning, Mel is on track and ready to go.

All because she decided to automate.

I admit there are a few things that don't fall into the Eliminate—Delegate—Automate system. Here's the final strategy to help alleviate pressure off you.

Negotiate

Often you can negotiate with the tasks you are asked to do for other people. If someone asks you to do something that you aren't great at—and you know you're not great at it—it's often best to tell the truth. Why is it so difficult to admit that you're just not good at it?

Once you admit your weakness, you can then negotiate using your brilliance. For example, perhaps your boss wants you to lead a highly visible project team. You feel flattered she asked you to take charge, but you know that your strength is co-leading teams, not being the sole leader. Having a co-leader maximizes your brilliance, and it's more enjoyable for you to work with a partner. Rather than just saying yes, you negotiate. You tell your boss that you know that more value could be added to this team if Hank—recommend someone by name—would co-lead the team with you. Nine times out of 10, the answer will be yes.

The same thing goes with your customers. Often customers will ask you to do projects or complete tasks that simply do not reflect your brilliance. Negotiate for another vendor to complete the project, work out a different result, or develop a new solution to the problem that reflects what you do best. Negotiation is a powerful tool if you use it to support what you do best.

The Power of Focus, if you really use it, will change how you work and live. It's all about making choices on how you spend your time. Spend it wisely, and you'll be successful for a long, long time. Spend it poorly, and . . . (you fill in the rest).

LIVING WITHOUT ADRENALINE

Another reason you may be unable to focus on what's most important in your life is because you're living on adrenaline. It's physically impossible for you to focus because you're buzzing around all day.

What a powerful drug you were born with! Adrenaline gives your body an extra burst of energy to help you get out of something. Like a car crash. A looming deadline. Putting out a fire. Handling all those crises in your life. Many of you reading this book use adrenaline the same way you use caffeine—as a way to get through the day at peak performance. You naturally produce the adrenaline hormone to keep you producing more and more work.

The problem with using too much adrenaline is it weakens your body. Using too much drains your energy. Why do you think you feel a tremendous down after spending the whole day charged up? It's because you weren't feeling high naturally. What goes up must come down.

Very often, you set up your life to keep getting the adrenaline. You put yourself in situations where you "have" to perform. You create dramas and crises so you'll be "forced" to give yourself that extra burst of energy to solve the problem. You overpromise something to someone so you'll be forced to meet a short deadline. The only way to make the deadline is to use crisis management.

That's usually why you just can't stop moving so fast to harness the power of focus. You're looking for the adrenaline to keep feeding you. You have to drive harder and move faster just to keep giving this natural drug to yourself. Yet you often tell yourself that you're moving so fast because you *have* to. The truth is you're stuck on adrenaline.

The big challenge with adrenaline is you cannot sustain the pace over time. You burn out. You feel stressed out. You tend to have high cycles of energy before you crash, so you feel you can't stop. Living on adrenaline forces you to lose control, and you lose the freedom you want so desperately in your life.

There are some of you who immediately said, "I don't have a problem with adrenaline." Maybe you need to take a closer look. Do people ever say these things about you?

- Boy, he is on all the time. How can his wife take it?
- I know she listened to what I said, but I don't think she heard me.
- You can always count on Jack to be late. That's just him.
- Karen is always so busy. What is she always doing?
- Jerry works too hard. What's with him?
- Why does Michelle put herself through all that stress? I think she likes it or something.

If this sounds like you, take the quiz on the following page to find out if adrenaline is a problem for you.

HOW TO BREAK THE ADRENALINE HABIT

I'm here to tell you there's an easier way. You'll be able to slow down without missing opportunities. You'll start to experience real, sustainable success, and you'll start to feel passion for your work again.

Let me use an example. I have a client—I'll call him Gary— who is a brilliant salesperson. He's the top-producing salesperson in his company, and he's always striving to top his last performance. When Gary hired me, he was burned out. He felt as if his life was being dictated by his customers, by his constantly ringing cellular phone, by his pager, and his voicemail that delivered more than 50 messages a day.

Whenever we were together, my heart would start racing. That's how charged up he was *all the time.* Yet Gary had another problem: He would deliberately tell his customers he could deliver a product before they needed it. Why? Because he

---

The Adrenaline Quiz

Circle **Y** for yes or **N** for no.

Do you drink caffeinated coffee or drinks to get or keep going?
Y   N

Do you eat sugar or smoke to calm yourself down?
Y   N

Do you tend to overpromise and then rush to get it done at the last minute?
Y   N

Do you find some way to sabotage a project, yet usually pull it off?
Y   N

Do you tend to take on more than you want because you feel you can?
Y   N

Do you react strongly to the unexpected?
Y   N

Do you find yourself getting very upset or annoyed (whether you show it or not) when people let you down, miss deadlines, or do less-than-optimal work? And do you take it personally?
Y   N

Do you arrive at work rushed or already on?
Y   N

Do you get grabbed by surprises or upsets and then not calm down for a day or more?
Y   N

Do you feel an inner rush or lack of stillness or peace much of the time?
Y   N

Are you the kind of person who tends to find the toughest way to get something done?
Y   N

Do you drive more than five miles over the speed limit, tail-gate, or criticize other drivers?
Y   N

Do you tend to run or arrive late, even if it's usually not your fault?
Y   N

Is money currently tight, but you can't seem to get ahead?
Y   N

Do you not give yourself plenty of time during your day for the things that may come up?
Y   N

Do you talk a lot even after people stop listening?
Y   N

Do you "people please" to the point of feeling compulsive, regardless of appropriateness or cost?
Y   N

If you answered yes to five or more of these, welcome to the club.

Adapted from a quiz produced by Thomas Leonard, founder of Coach University, www.coachu.com. Used with permission.

thought his task was to exceed expectations, even if he knew the company couldn't deliver. That didn't matter to Gary. He figured he'd find a way to deliver anyway. And he usually did—by working 15 hours a day doing the work himself.

Adrenaline!

So you're ready to break your adrenaline habit? Good. Let me give you a few ideas that will help you shatter your old way of performing. It's not easy to break your adrenaline habit, but with some patience and hard work, it can happen.

Stop Drinking Caffeine and Eating Sugar

Eliminate all caffeine and sugar products. That means you switch to decaffeinated coffee. No more midmorning stops at the coffee pot. No more midafternoon candy bars or sodas to keep you moving. Mixing caffeine and adrenaline is vicious. It's a constant, never-ending cycle to keep you up. It's time to shift into feeling up without artificial means.

Expect withdrawal from not having caffeine anymore. The first couple of days or weeks, you're going to get a headache from the withdrawal, and you may feel groggy. That's part of kicking the habit.

If you're drinking five cups of coffee a day, reduce your intake to four cups for a few days. Then reduce it to three, then to two, and then to one cup. You can do the same thing by alternating caffeinated and decaf coffee. Start with integrating one cup of decaf coffee until you're only drinking decaf coffee. The same thing goes with any products that have caffeine in them.

When I was writing this book in 1997, my husband was traveling an awful lot for his job. Whenever he's away, I have a very difficult time sleeping. I usually survive on just a few hours a night until he comes home. Thankfully, he's typically gone only two nights a week—and that's rare these days.

On one trip, he was gone for three weeks. How does someone survive for three weeks of not sleeping? My answer was caffeine.

At around 2 P.M. every day, I would start to feel groggy. I'm like you, and I have a lot to do during my days, so I would fill my water bottle up with Coke. I'd drink caffeine all afternoon and be so wired on it, I couldn't sleep at night. The cycle would start all over again the next day. I know if I would just have adjusted to his leave naturally, I would easily have started sleeping normally after a few days, but instead I dove into a caffeine-rich world. Never again.

Drink water instead.

Leave 15 Minutes *Early* for Every Appointment

And I mean every appointment. The problem with folks on adrenaline is they unconsciously leave late so they'll have to speed off to their appointments and get that rush. You know what it's like to come barreling in the conference room door. You get noticed.

The challenge is you're already charged up. You spend the first 10 minutes trying to get your thoughts and your breathing under control from having to rush over. Being charged up prevents you from paying attention to what's really going on around you. You fail to listen to what's happening, and there's a great chance you'll miss opportunities because you weren't tuned in. Missed opportunities reduce your chances of working less and making more.

Stop Meeting with People After 1 P.M.

What happens to most of you is you meet with people from the minute you walk into the office until the minute you get home. Have you ever noticed that meeting with people takes a lot of energy from you? If your calendar is jammed with meetings, you have spent most of the afternoon high on adrenaline just to get through your schedule.

Your family gets to experience the crash when you walk in the front door. One of the reasons you feel exhausted when you come home is because you've been charged up on adrenaline all day. Stopping all your appointments by 1 P.M. gives you four hours to settle down off the adrenaline high before you go home. Try it. It works.

Underpromise Everything. Overdeliver Everything

I know you're starting to panic right now. "How can I under-promise to my clients and customers?" You can. Think back to the story I told you earlier about Gary. He thought exceeding his customers' expectations was about telling them he'd deliver earlier than they wanted. The real truth is exceeding their expectations comes from overdelivering, not overpromising. Talk is cheap. Prove that you care about them and their business not by overpromising, but by overdelivering.

The greatest thing about underpromising is it gives you a sense of ease. You know you can deliver easily so you eliminate the need to rush to get something done. That's a key point of working less and making more.

Here's how it works: You're finalizing your customer's orders, and they ask you when they will receive their product or service. You know you can rush and deliver the project by Monday. If you had until Tuesday, you would give yourself a realistic time frame to complete the work. If you waited to deliver until Thursday, you would have built in time just in case something went wrong. So you ask your customer, "Will Thursday be okay?" They say sure. Everything goes as planned, and you deliver on Tuesday. You've exceeded your customer's expectations by 48 hours by under-promising and overdelivering. And you still had two extra days built in to handle any problems that could have come up.

Spend 80 Percent of Your Time Listening and 20 Percent of Your Time Talking

Forcing yourself to listen to other people will enable you to shift out of what you're feeling and into what they're saying. People who are stuck on adrenaline spend all the time talking. A great way to shatter your adrenaline habit is to stop talking and start listening.

You'll find yourself paying attention to what's going on around you rather than getting caught up in the adrenaline high you're on. When you stop to listen, you begin to hear what's really happening, and you may notice that you've been missing some crucial details. Those vital details may be just the thing you need to work less and make more. Force yourself to slow down to pay attention. You can only pay attention when you stop talking and start listening.

Stop Believing You Can Pull It Off, and Give Yourself Some Time

The main reason you're so charged up on adrenaline is probably because you believe that you work well under pressure. Okay, so you've trained yourself to be the hero and do things at the last minute. You probably do it all the time, push the envelope so you have to stay up until 2 A.M. to get it done.

Do not be fooled. You do not do better work under pressure. You probably do okay work under pressure, and you're such an achiever that your okay work is better than everyone else's. But it's not your best work. If you want to Work Less, Make More, you must build in extra time to get it done right. Get it done to the best of your ability. Stop undermining massive success by just doing it okay, good enough to get by.

Reorganize your calendar so you get projects done 48 hours before they are due. Every time. You'll find those extra two days allow you to put your own unique spin and style on the project so you end up doing outstanding work, not just good work.

You can pull it off. But what I want is for you to become a master at the work you do. And you need to give yourself time to go for mastery.

BUILD A SYSTEM TO SUPPORT YOU

You've just read through the first three steps of the Work Less, Make More program. For some of you, there's a question that's still burning. "What if I want a life where I can have it all? I want the money. I want a great career. I want a family. I want to travel. I want to drive a fancy sports car and live in an expensive house. I want to do it all. How can I do it all when my schedule is already jammed?"

If you're overcommitted, you have extremely high standards for your life. You want to live life to the fullest, so you get involved in a lot of different things. Work Less, Make More is not about lowering your standards. It's not about believing it when people say, "You expect too much." You don't expect too much from life, but you probably expect too much from yourself. Working less and making more is about making your life easier. It's about making it effortless, and it simply can't be effortless if you're overcommitted. Having too much to do adds more stress in your life. It doesn't add ease and comfort.

What you forgot to do is build a system to support your lifestyle. That's really what the power of focus is all about: having the right resources and people in place so you can focus on what matters the most to give you the results you want.

Most people forget to upgrade their resources when they upgrade their lifestyle, and then they can't figure out what's taking all their time. When you grow, unless you build in the resources to support your growth, you will feel overcommitted. Guaranteed.

For example, you start making enough money to move into the home of your dreams. It has twice the square footage you're used to, but you know you can easily afford the monthly mortgage payments. You're moving up in the world, so you move in. Once you've been there a few months, you realize your new home takes more than just money. It takes time, a lot more time than your old home. Someone has to clean the house. Someone has to garden and keep up the lawn. Someone has to take care of maintenance. Someone has to buy furniture and redecorate. These things take longer because your new home is simply bigger than your old one.

You've added more than just a new house into your life. You need time to invest in its upkeep. You feel overwhelmed because you didn't build a system to support your new environment.

To move into a new home without its taking any more time requires that you hire a cleaning service, a lawn service, and a maintenance service as a minimum. To get the full advantage of the house without its taking any more time, you'll want a gardener, a grocery shopping service, a window washer, a plumber, an electrician, and a service to do your laundry. Problem is, you didn't think about that when you moved in because you were focused only on upgrading your home. Anytime you upgrade anything, it always takes time, energy, and passion to operate efficiently. It's no wonder your calendar is jammed.

The same thing is true for your office. You upgraded your computer system, but you forgot to add in time to learn the new system. You didn't think you'd need a computer technician, so you spend wasteful hours trying to learn it yourself. Maybe you send one staff member to training, and you expect that person to train everyone else and still complete his or her job responsibilities. But the star member can't do it all, so you pick up some of the slack. After all, you're ultimately responsible for the task's getting done.

This is not the way to live. In fact, a few years ago, simplifying your life became a very powerful theme. You could actually let go of the things that weren't important—like the big mortgage, expensive cars, demanding careers—for a more simple life. For some people, the simplification process was the answer they were searching for. For many people who still wanted it all, simplification was not the answer. Your answer may be building a system that supports you.

Go through your life and look at where you can build a strong system to support your new lifestyle. Feeling overcommitted is an indication that you failed to build a system for what you have, what you do, and who you have become.

Learning to harness the Power of Focus is a vital part of Work Less, Make More. You've been given the road map to use this powerful tool. Are you using it to make more of your life?

Exercises

1. Write down your top three payoff activities. What are the specific actions you're going to take this week to spend 80 percent of your time doing these activities? Pull out your calendar and schedule it in.

2. Go back to the list you made of the stuff that takes up your time. Pick out one activity and delegate it to someone else this week. Take at least one hour to train that person to complete the task to your standards.

3. Where in your life are you overcommitted? Pay close attention to why your schedule is so packed. Brainstorm in your journal this week how you can use the Power of Three to refocus your priorities.

4. Where in your life have you failed to build a strong support system? Are you doing too much at home? At the office? In your free time? Use your journal to explore the ways you can build a powerful system to support what you have, what you do, and who you are.

5. What are the areas in your life where you're weak? You know, the stuff you do poorly. Identify what qualities a person needs to have in order to handle these tasks. Then go out and add them to your support team.

6. Pull out your journal. What is your purpose of being? Who are your current customers? Your future customers? Be very clear on defining these three areas in your life. They are the basis for using the power of three.

7. Kick the adrenaline habit this week. Stop drinking coffee. Stop rushing off to meetings. Stop meeting with people after 1 P.M. Do anything this week to shift into a different way of operating. Ask yourself, "How is my life different when I'm not using adrenaline to get everything done?"

CHAPTER 4

Handle the
Time Machine

I once heard someone say something that made a lot of sense: "Time is more important than money. If you run out of money, you can always get more. If you run out of time, you can't get any more."

Time is the most valuable commodity you have. I know that deep inside your gut you believe if you could only get a handle on how you manage time, then everything would be all right. If you even knew how many phone calls I get from people asking me if we can help them be better time managers.

The truth is that time management is an oxymoron. No matter what you do, you can't manage time. You can't control how fast it moves. You can't slow it down or speed it up. You can't stop time. All you can do is control how you show up in time.

Yet you often fool yourself about time. You like to pretend that the tempo of your days is not your own. You think someone or something else is making you feel frazzled and stressed out. You're constantly getting caught up in the tidal wave of things that have to get done, and you're out of control.

I know, I know. You're asking yourself, "How can time be my own?" You're thinking about family obligations, business responsibilities, and a whole slew of other reasons why you can't get a handle on your time. The fact is, how you spend your time is up to you. Why is it that you miraculously find the time to do what you want to do?

Work Less, Make More is learning how to love the life that you created. It's your life. It doesn't belong to your spouse, your parents, your teachers, your mentors, your coaches, your bosses, your kids, or anyone else. It belongs to you.

Make yourself the priority. Take back control. This sounds like a dramatic thing—like quitting your job, giving up your drive to make money, and moving to a cabin in the mountains, alone.

Put aside this drama. There is a very simple, very effective way to make time your own: by saying yes to yourself and to what really counts.

REORGANIZING YOUR DAYS

One of the single best ways to take back control is to use the Power of Three and how you organize what you do during a day. This system is about letting the tidal wave flow right over you while you stay strong and in control.

The problem that you probably face is you're bombarded with tons of things to do every single day. If you're like most people, you find yourself moving from one thing to another to another all day long. Your mind is constantly shifting from one project to something else, and you're unable to concentrate and harness your brilliance because you never gain enough momentum.

That's why you often feel like you haven't gotten anything done at the end of the day. You haven't built momentum to create results. Work Less, Make More is all about results. If you deliver results, your customers don't care if you work two hours a day or 12 hours a day. If you deliver results, your employer will promote you even if you take all your vacation days or if you leave early on Tuesdays to coach your son's baseball team. When you deliver results, you decide how much you'll work and how much you'll get paid.

The problem is if you're not using your time to get results, you'll never Work Less, Make More. Never.

The answer is not to spend a tremendous amount of time learning how to use your calendar or planner. You don't have to sit in a day-long seminar to learn a simple system I teach my clients to help them create momentum.

All you have to do is use the Power of Three System to do less and achieve more. It's as easy as giving each day a theme.

Let me explain how this works. Every one of you has a variety of things you focus on in your job. If you sit back and look at all the things you have to do, you'll notice they fall into specific categories. For example, you have a need to spend time in administration, strategic planning, creative problem solving, business development, political maneuvering, communications, financial issues, long-term opportunities, and managing your staff. There's probably stuff you deal with that I haven't even identified.

The challenge is most people try to juggle each one of their responsibilities and cram them into one day. You do paperwork, then meet with your staff, then go to lunch with a client, then spend two hours in a meeting with a vendor. And don't forget about returning voicemail and e-mail messages. You're trying to do too many different things each day.

This way of operating is ludicrous. You can't build momentum if you're trying to do everything every day. So the answer is to decide what three days you want to have, and build everything into those specific days.

Let me show you what many coaches teach their clients to do. By using the Power of Three, I direct my clients to have three types of days: Laser Days, Support Days, and Free Days.

Laser Days

I call these Laser Days because I want you to focus like a laser on what matters the most: your Power of Three. Nothing else matters on Laser Days except these three things.

Go back to Chapter 3 and identify the top three most important activities you do. I call these your high-payoff activities. The three most important things you just can't seem to find the time to do. This is the stuff that if you simply spent eight hours a day working on, you'd find yourself making a lot more money and getting better results. (We spend a lot of time on this in Chapter 3. Go back and do the work if you haven't already completed it. This won't mean anything unless you have a real example to work with.)

On Laser Days, *all* you do is these three things. Nothing else. From the time you show up at the office to the time you go home, you focus all your attention on these three activities.

Many times you're not getting the results you want because you're unable to focus long enough to achieve them. By spending a big block of time on your high-payoff activities, you'll start to build momentum. What you'll achieve as a result of this momentum will be enormous. Schedule as many focus days as possible each week.

For example, if you own your business, your Laser Days will be exclusively reserved for meeting with potential customers, working on long-term profit projects, and developing strong relationships with your current customers. You won't spend time on anything else. Not one useless meeting. Not one phone call to your staff—unless it has to do with a high-payoff activity you're doing at that very moment. Focus on the top three high-impact activities all day.

You'll find yourself on Laser Days developing new and innovative approaches to what you're doing. You'll find yourself solving problems before they even become problems. You'll find yourself doing three, four, sometimes five more times the amount of work than you usually do. The results will come in faster and faster because you're spending your time wisely.

Start with at least two Laser Days each week until you gradually spend 80 percent of your time doing Focus activities.

Support Days

Support Days are for getting all the work done that you generated on your Laser Days. Follow-up activities. Administrative stuff. Paperwork. Committee meetings. You get the idea. Support Days are also the perfect days to set up meetings with your staff—if you have any—and to meet with vendors. Do *not* use your Laser Days to handle Support activities. Go back to the list of all the stuff that prevents you from doing great work. These are the perfect Support activities.

If you're a salesperson, your Support Days should be spent putting together proposals, quotes, and handling customer service issues. Spend your Support Days taking care of all the work you created on your Laser Days. You'll probably spend the majority of your time in the office on these days.

Your Support Days will be used in conjunction with delegation. As you're learning how to become a master delegator, there are activities you'll need to do until you can find the right person to do the work and then train them how to do it. At first, you'll find yourself having a lot of Support Days. Over time, you'll gradually spend 20 percent of your time on these types of activities.

Free Days

Free Days are just what they sound like: FREE Days. That means no work. Not one phone call. Not one e-mail. Not even voicemail. Do nothing that has to do with work. If you spend any time working, it is *not* a Free Day. Use this time for play. Have fun. Enjoy the hobbies in your life. Spend time with the people who are important to you. Play golf. Go shopping. Putter around in the garden. Do activities you like to do that are not related to work. Schedule at least two Free Days a week.

Free Days are vital to your life. They allow you to leave your work behind and replenish who you are. If you're working all the time, you don't give yourself the opportunity to cultivate the other parts of yourself. You'll soon find yourself burned out and unable to work. Yes, even if your work is your passion. You need time off. Free Days allow you to find fulfillment outside your work.

What about all those activities that don't fit into Support or Laser days? Take them off your To-Do list. Get rid of them—permanently. They aren't bringing any value to you, so eliminate them from your life.

Your assignment: Pull out your calendar and start planning for your Laser, Support, and Free days. I use color-coded highlighters to keep my calendar on track. Yellow is for Laser Days. Green is for Support Days, and blue is for Free Days. Once a month, sit down and identify what day will be which type of day. Then stick by your new system.

Most of the clients I work with feel extremely relieved when they learn this easy-to-understand system. It seems easy and effortless to implement. But don't be fooled. It takes some practice to get the system to work right for you. Take Ronald, for example. Ronald owns a business and has five managers who report directly to him. When he first started implementing this system, he was on fire. During the first week alone, Ronald was able to focus on some much-needed, long-term opportunities, and he took major strides in developing a relationship with a potential partner. Weeks later, we discovered that the work he had done that week gave him a $50,000 payoff.

Everything was going great until a crisis happened at work. Ronald rushed in to solve the problem, and he struggled to get back on the system for the next 30 days. When the program was new, Ronald told me it was easier to implement. Yet when a monkey wrench was thrown in—as they always are—the system broke down for him.

What Ronald had failed to do was allow himself to work with the program over a period of time. It's not ever going to be perfect. You're putting in a new operating system, and you need to tweak the system to fit your needs.

Now just because I recommend that my clients use three specific types of days doesn't mean you can't vary from the system. Perhaps you need one day a week where all you focus on is creative solutions. Call it your Creative Day. Or maybe you need two days a week to handle some financial issues for the next few months. Make those your Money Days.

One of my associates, Chuck Proudift, plans a Business Planning Day once a quarter to help him stay on course with his long-term vision. Chuck sits down for eight hours and reviews his business plan to see where he's on track and where he needs some work. Then he invests his day refocusing and redesigning how he operates. How powerful would it be if you did that?

My point is you must use your time to create momentum, and the single best way to do it is categorize what you do on a specific day so you can get results. Remember, Work Less, Make More is all about results. And when you deliver results, you decide how much you'll work and how much you'll get paid.

TIPS THAT MAKE THIS SYSTEM WORK

Communicate with the People Around You

Before you implement the Power of Three System, you must sit down and have a conversation with your support team. It's crucial that you communicate what you're doing with your team and ask them to support you.

That means your assistant doesn't schedule meetings with anyone on your Laser Days. Your staff doesn't pop into your office on your Laser Days. Your family doesn't schedule doctors' appointments or midday errands on your Laser Days. Keep a calendar at home and at the office so everyone will know what type of day you're working on. Ask them to respect you and your schedule, and let them know you have built in time on Support and Free days just for them.

Stay True to Working a Full Day on Each Type of Day

The first question my clients ask me is if they can combine the type of days. For example, they want to spend four hours on Laser Day activities in the morning and four hours on Support activities in the afternoon. Or they want to spend four hours on Support activities and four hours on Free time.

If you divide your attention during any given day, you are dramatically reducing your chance of success. Remember, this system is about building momentum. The second that you take your attention away from the task at hand, you stop yourself from moving forward. It takes at least 10 minutes for you to get back into the flow once you've turned your attention back to the task. For some people, their whole day is shot if they lose focus. Harness the power of focus by being true to this system. Do not divide your attention between different days.

Focus on Current and Future Opportunities on Your Laser Days

Support Days are easy to fill up. You have plenty of paperwork, meetings, and administrative work to get done. Most people right now have too many Support Days on their schedules. Some people spend every day, day after day, on Support activities. The trick to Work Less, Make More is what you do on a Laser Day.

You're not used to spending an entire eight hours focused on your most important activities. It takes time to train yourself what to do on these days. At first, you may find yourself searching for things to do on your Laser Days. That's perfectly okay, but stay true to the system. Force yourself to focus.

A good rule of thumb is to divide your Laser Days between two types of activities: current revenues and future revenues. Each and every one of you has activities and projects that affect current revenues for your company. If you don't directly have influence, like a salesperson or entrepreneur would, you influence someone who influences someone who influences someone who has a direct impact on current revenues. Fifty percent of your time needs to be focused on current customers who are paying you within the next 90 days. That's what I call focusing on current revenues.

The other 50 percent of your Laser Days needs to be spent on future opportunities. These are projects that will bring in revenues after the next 90 days. Focusing on your future endeavors ensures you're building a lifetime of business for yourself and for the company. A future revenues focus helps you to identify and take advantage of opportunities you would have missed had you spent all your time on Support activities.

What I typically see are people who spend too much time on Support, and they feel as if they are never getting anything done. They aren't. On the other end of the spectrum, I see people who spend so much time on future revenues that they forget to take care of their current customers and their current cash flow. They invariably go out of business—or spend their lives on the adrenaline treadmill—because they weren't able to meet their short-term cash demands.

You can do both by simply dividing your Laser Days between current revenues and future revenues activities.

Be Flexible

Keep in mind that you need to experiment for a while with the Power of Three System. It's impossible for me to explain all the different nuances of the system without knowing your specific situation. You must be flexible. Use and constantly fine-tune this system to fit who you are and what is going on in your life.

WHAT TO DO ON YOUR FREE DAYS

One of the classic problems many people face is what to do with the time that's freed up in their days. When you begin to Work Less, Make More, you may feel uneasy because you have a lot more time on your hands. I know, that's exactly what you're looking for. The problem is you've been making yourself so busy that you've forgotten what having free time is all about. You may feel a bit *insane* for a while, and you may find yourself walking around not sure what to do.

It's important to decide what it is you want to do on your Free Days. Start imagining how you'll spend your time when you have enough to do what you really want. It's often hard for you to even imagine having more time. You never spend the time to decide how you'll spend your days if they were exactly how you wanted them. That's the reason you never seem to find yourself with any free time. In order for you to create Free Days, you need a reason to do so. What do you want to do during your time off?

This may be a difficult task for you to complete. I consulted with my first Work Less, Make More coaching group, and I challenged them to come up with a huge list of things to do on their Free Days. On the page opposite is just a sampling of what they came up with.

Get the idea? Put down this book, create your own list in your journal, and then go out and do something fun. Do something for no reason other than you just want to. Come up with your own ideas or take a few ideas from this list.

ON THE PLATE VERSUS ON THE SCHEDULE

Another vital tool in handling the time machine is taking care of all that stuff on your plate. You've heard people—maybe yourself—say, "I have so much on my plate right now." On your plate are all the projects, activities, and tasks that you committed to spending time on, but never seem to get around to completing. These things show up on your To Do list day after day, but most of them are never handled. They stay on the plate until there's a deadline forcing you to do them.

What about moving all this stuff to your schedule? Get it off your plate and on your schedule so you'll actually get it done. For example, you agree to put together a proposal for a prospect, and they want the proposal by next Friday. It's Monday, and you tell yourself you have all week to do it. Surely you'll find the time to get to it. So it goes on your To Do list. Tuesday comes along, and you put it on your daily action list. Wednesday comes along, and it's still not done because something else got in the way.

What to Do on a Free Day

• Spend time with my family, just laughing and having fun.

• Go shopping *without a purpose or a list.*

• Spend Sunday afternoon leafing through catalogs.

• Take a bubble bath in the Jacuzzi.

• Go wine tasting at a vineyard.

• Go to an art auction.

• Paint a picture.

• Try calligraphy.

• Learn how to speak Spanish.

• Sit on the lawn watching butterflies.

• Lie in the sun.

• Listen to a great CD.

• Walk around the block.

• Read a book I've always wanted to read.

• Write a book I've always wanted to write.

• Read a trashy romance novel.

• Write a love letter to my spouse.

• Take photos of nature.

• Go out to lunch with a friend.

• Explore the city.

• Practice Zen meditation.

• Play my guitar.

(Continued)

What to Do on a Free Day (Continued)

- Go jogging.

- Build a water garden.

- Spend two hours in a bookstore *without* feeling guilty.

- Talk to my mom or dad on the phone.

- Go for a hike in the woods.

- Have a picnic.

- Surf the Web for fun stuff.

- Daydream.

- Read all those coffee table books I never spend much time with.

- Make chocolate covered anythings and eat them slowly.

- Paint terra cotta pots.

- Build a snowperson, or a whole community of snowpeople and snowpets.

- Make my own perfume.

- Snuggle with my spouse.

- Make jewelry.

- Hug a tree.

- Go to a thrift store.

- Meditate.

- Play card games.

- Draw dinosaurs.

Thursday comes along, and it's 3 P.M. You're freaked out because you needed your assistant's help, and he had to leave at 4 P.M. for a doctor's appointment. You stay up the whole night to complete it, but it's certainly not your best work. You got it done, but with a lot of stress, anxiety, and regrets. Does any of this sound strangely familiar?

Instead, when you decide to take on a new project or task, immediately open up your calendar and schedule in the time to get it done. On Monday, you can look at Tuesday and notice you have a two-hour break between meetings (it's a Support Day), so you schedule in two hours to complete the proposal. You then write a quick note to your assistant letting him know your part of the proposal will be done by 4 P.M. on Tuesday, and you need the completed document in your hands no later than Wednesday at 5 P.M. That gives you an entire day to review the proposal and request any changes that need to be made.

When it's on the schedule, it gets done. When it's on the plate, it may never get done.

What do you have on your plate? Take an inventory of all the things you've committed to accomplishing and schedule the time to do them. Yes, I know there are some of you who have numerous projects on your plate, and if you scheduled them all, it would be jammed for the next three weeks. So be it. It's time to clean off your plate so you can take advantage of new opportunities without feeling guilty that you're leaving something undone.

The beauty of using the "on the schedule" strategy is it allows you to control your work day. If someone calls you to participate in a project, you can immediately look at your schedule and negotiate the deadline. You don't have to say no right away. In fact, if you do say yes and put something else on your plate without putting it on your schedule, you'll rush around at the last minute to get it done. You'll probably do a less-than-great job and the benefit you would have derived from the situation simply would not be there.

Use your schedule to control your day rather than letting your day control you.

PROCRASTINATION

Okay, you're telling yourself. Dividing my days into three types sounds like a good thing, and so does shifting from having things on my plate to on my schedule. "I'll get around to doing it tomorrow," you tell yourself.

A big block to Work Less, Make More is procrastination. You know, putting your life on hold because you're just not ready to take action. Does this sound like you?

- I have lots of things I want to accomplish, but I hate all those details.
- My boss asked me to do the assignment, but why do I have to do it?
- I know what to do, but I need to do more research—just to make sure.
- I see everyone around me achieving their goals, but I'm afraid to change.
- I could do that important assignment, but I get motivated only at the last minute.
- I have great ideas, big dreams, but I have so much to do.

Did you notice the use of the word *but* in these statements?

You may have good intentions for changing your life, yet you never seem to get around to living your life. Rather than *doing* things, you spend your time *obsessing* about why you aren't doing them. What I mean by obsessing is that you spend your time going around and around in your head why you're not doing something. Yes, you know a project needs to get done. Yes, you want to take action. No, you just don't do it. You say things like: "I don't feel like doing it now." "I'll get to it tomorrow." "There is too much to do." This obsessing doesn't do any good. It only makes things worse because you're focused on how you're failing, not on how you're succeeding.

Procrastination, obviously, can be a big problem. You can't redesign your life if you're not able to take action. A part of handling the time machine is eliminating procrastination from your life and gaining back control of your schedule. More like taking back control.

Let me help you take back control. Procrastination isn't just about what you do. So often you fall into the trap of believing that you just need to get more organized or you just need to learn how to manage your time better. It's more than that. Much more. No matter how organized you are or how much you learn how to manage your time, you're not dealing with the source of your procrastination. You're just treating the symptoms, and this approach will ultimately fail.

Procrastination is about how you *think,* how you *speak,* and how you *act.* All three work together to block you from having more success in your life. Changing how you think, speak, and act can help you unblock the procrastination that holds you back from working less and making more.

Changing How You Think

The best way to change how you think is to take responsibility for everything that happens in your life. And I mean *everything.* Most procrastinators blame everyone else for imposing deadlines, asking them to do the work, and waiting until the last minute to give assignments. To change how you think, you must take responsibility. You procrastinate, and it's not anyone else's fault but your own. Only you can change your behavior.

One of my clients, Mary, had a big problem with procrastination. When we first started working together, Mary had blamed everyone else for her procrastination. She couldn't finish an assignment because her boss had not signed the paperwork. She couldn't clean up her house because her son was off at college, and his room was a disaster. She couldn't find a new job, because she was waiting for her husband to get information on their pension plan. It was always someone else's fault, but not her own.

I challenged Mary to take ultimate responsibility for her life.

"How is it serving you to blame everyone else for your procrastination?" I asked her one day. She didn't know the answer right off the bat, but after a few weeks, she came back and told me her truth.

"When I blame other people for my problems," Mary said, "I give in to my fear of moving forward. I'm afraid that if I do take action, my whole life will change in a way I don't want. I'm afraid of what will happen, and I'm comfortable being right where I am." The truth was she wasn't happy where she was, but her fear was greater than her ability to move forward.

Telling the truth to yourself and taking full responsibility for what isn't working is the first key to undoing procrastination from your life.

Changing How You Speak

There are two big words that affect how you feel, especially about yourself and about procrastination. BUT and SHOULD. Think about it. *I should do it, but I don't want to. I should help Joe, but I'm too busy. I should . . . , but . . .*

Eliminate these words from your vocabulary. Stop saying *should* and *but*. Instead of using the word *should*, use the word *want*. Instead of using the word *but*, use the word *and*. For example, *I want to do it, and I don't want to. I want to help Joe, and I am too busy.* Make the commitment to eliminate all the *should*s and *but*s from your life.

*Should*s are especially damaging. For example: *I should lose weight. I should make 10 cold calls a day. I should love my mean boss. I should do more.* The *should*s in our lives are usually there because we want to please someone else. Losing weight? Maybe your spouse keeps nagging you to get healthy. Until you're ready to lose weight, forget it. Same thing with organizing.

Few of us graduate to a place in life where we truly make our own choices. Most of us are bound by what we have been told is the truth, the *should*s in our lives. What about your own truth?

What I want for you is to design your life around what you want to do, what you love to do. You have the luxury of designing your life exactly as you want it, not as your parents had it, not like others live theirs.

I challenge you to do only the things you want to do. Yeah, I know, a big challenge. Don't get caught in the trap of thinking all you want to do is lie around and eat chocolate all day. I don't believe it. What about spending time with people who appreciate you? Mastering your craft to the point that you're adding to it? Designing your life around what you really want? That's what I'm talking about. Focus on what you want to do, not all the *shoulds*, *coulds*, and *ought tos*.

That's what Work Less, Make More is about. Doing what you want to do, not what you think you should do.

Changing How We Act

Behavior has a lot to do with procrastination. After we have changed how we think and how we speak, the next logical step is to change how we act.

Write It Down

Every time you find yourself procrastinating about something, take the time to write it down. Reflect on the problem. Ask yourself a few questions: Why am I procrastinating? What don't I want to do? Is there another way to get this done without doing it myself?

Break a Big Project into Small Pieces

You've probably heard this one before, but often the reason you procrastinate is because the task seems overwhelming. Rather than look at the whole project, schedule one hour every day to chip away at what needs to get done. Just a little bit every day. If you procrastinate until the last minute on a big project, you'll *really* feel overwhelmed.

Ask for Help

Seems easy enough, but often you procrastinate because you just don't want to do it yourself. Please, ask for help. Mary, the client I told you about before, kept procrastinating about cleaning up the clutter in her office. I recommended she delegate the task to her assistant, rather than force herself to do it. Now on Friday afternoons, her assistant comes into her office and reorganizes it. The work is done, and Mary has freed herself up from constantly procrastinating about it. She no longer feels guilty leaving a messy office because she knows it'll be handled on Friday afternoons.

Turn Your Work into Fun

Often, you procrastinate because the task seems boring. Really boring. Put your creativity to work. Make a contest or a game out of the task if it seems too dreary. For example, give yourself just 15 minutes to complete a task. Set the timer, then rush around to get as much done as you possibly can. This works really well if you're procrastinating on cleaning up your office. See how much you can clean up in 15 minutes. Develop your own games to help you get your tasks done.

Give Yourself a Reward

I know it sounds like you're one of Pavlov's dogs, but sometimes you just may need a reward for getting something done. Why not reward yourself with an ice cream cone after you've cleaned out your closets? Or a night out on the town when you've completed that huge project at work?

The reward system worked extremely well for one of my friends. Susie was starting a new business, and she was getting a bit depressed because the money wasn't coming in as fast as she wanted. I recommended that Susie put up a white board and keep track of her daily activities, rather than focusing on the result. If she did the necessary business-building tasks day after day, I knew her results would come.

Susie loved the idea, and she even set up a reward system for herself. Her first goal was to accumulate enough points so that she could "afford" a cleaning service for her home. The reward was based on what she did on a daily basis, not on the results she got. She didn't procrastinate on these crucial tasks because she knew the payoff was something she wanted. Every time Susie's cleaning service cleans her house, she celebrates the work she's done.

Make Sure Your Delays Are Truly Procrastination

Some of you may have falsely labeled yourselves as procrastinators. You may procrastinate because you need time to let new ideas settle in and simmer. You're creative beings, and you're constantly developing new ideas and new strategies to make your life more meaningful. Sometimes that means you need to take ideas and let them settle for a while. Don't beat yourself up about procrastinating if what you're really doing is creating. There's a big difference.

When I was writing this book, I set up a discipline to write two chapters a week, and I scheduled the time into my calendar. When that time came up, I sat down at the computer, and I made a habit out of writing this book. Sometimes, though, I just couldn't write. I had to let the ideas simmer for a while before I could put my thoughts on paper. I would take my dogs for a walk, write in my journal, or just lie on my bed and rest. From the outside, I looked like I was procrastinating, but what I was really doing was being creative. Giving myself time and space to develop an idea. It's up to you to know the difference. Work Less, Make More is about taking action. If you aren't taking action, you need to find out why so you can change your behavior.

Note: If you're a chronic procrastinator, if this is really a big problem for you, working with a trained therapist can help you explore why you've been using procrastination. Please ask for help if you need it.

PERFECTIONISM

There's another big block that has everything to do with handling the time machine, and it often goes hand in hand with procrastination. It's called *perfectionism*. I find most of the folks who are interested in Work Less, Make More find themselves caught in the perfectionist trap from time to time.

What's wrong with trying to be perfect? Perfectionism certainly seems like an honorable goal. Yet the sad reality is that trying to be perfect sabotages your efforts.

Perfectionism is not about being right or doing it right. Your quest for perfection actually holds you back. Going for perfect forces you to go for "all or nothing." Many times what you get is nothing. This extreme attitude stops you from feeling good about your performance. You'll never reach perfection, so you can't enjoy anything you do. No matter how much you achieve, it's never enough.

For perfectionists, failing at a task does not mean the task wasn't performed successfully. It means who they are is a failure. Their self-esteem is so tightly tied to being perfect that failure proves to them they are inadequate and worthless. Too much criticism can be paralyzing, so they stop moving forward. They certainly can't design a life that allows them to work less and make more.

One of my past clients, Lori Stine, came up with a great list that describes perfectionists in the workplace. Do any of those on the facing page sound like you?

I know, when put this way, it seems ridiculous to be so focused on being perfect. Most of my clients have an issue with perfectionism. Like Steven.

Steven is what you call a high achiever. He can do a lot of things, and he can do most of them tremendously well. He used to do his own copying, his own typing, his own mailings. He worked on every meticulous detail in his business, and he did them extremely well. He even cut his own grass, and when he was finished, it looked like a professional gardener had done it.

What's the problem? Steven was always working. Nothing was ever "right," and even though he kept working at it, he never seemed to get it perfect. Getting it right in his book was getting it perfect. So he kept beating his head against the wall and worked

You Know You're a Perfectionist When . . .

- You use your spell check program, don't trust it, and end up looking up words in your dictionary anyway.

- You stare at a blank page, or a blank screen, for five minutes before you begin to write anything.

- Your personal letters are the culmination of a first draft and three rewrites.

- You address an envelope before discovering that it is upside down, and throw it out because you just can't send it.

- You throw out an addressed and stamped envelope upon realizing that the stamp is either upside down or crooked.

- You can't imagine sending personal correspondence with a leftover holiday postage stamp any time after December 25th.

- You rewrite an entire sentence just because you've gotten to a word that you don't know how to spell and you're not in the mood to look it up.

- You write an e-mail when you're pressed for time, stating that you're in a hurry and that you're not going to proofread it before sending it out, but you proceed to proofread it anyway.

more hours. He freely admitted he was not enjoying his life. Steven's perfectionist tendencies forced him to spend time on unimportant things, and that caused him to work twice as long as anyone else. Yet with all the time he was investing, he wasn't getting twice the return.

Steven hired me to help him create more free time in his life. The first thing he had to do was give up going for perfect. We settled on going for excellent instead. Like Steve, you must break the debilitating loop that perfectionism brings. Learn what needs to be right, what needs to be your personal best, and what will be okay just being okay. It's a balance you'll need to create for yourself.

What can you do to stop striving to be so perfect?

Focus on What's Realistic versus What's Perfect

When you do something, don't get caught up in thinking about the best possible way. Instead, come up with several options. There's not one perfect way; there are lots of different ways. Once you've developed your options, you can choose the one that works the best for you.

Perfectionists tend to have an all-or-nothing attitude. Break that cycle by coming up with at least three options for every task, activity, and project you can complete.

Give Yourself a Time Line to Complete a Task and Stick By It

This was a big change Steven made. He shifted from doing perfect work to doing excellent work within a given time. When Steven was working on a project he thought would take two hours, he set a timer for 120 minutes. When the timer beeped, he had to stop doing any more work on that activity. Whatever work he had done up to that point was good enough.

This was a huge breakthrough for Steven. He learned that spending hundreds of hours on unnecessary tasks was not going to help him work less and make more. By developing time limitations on his work, he was able to divert his attention away from perfect to doing excellent work.

Have a Healthy Relationship with Failure

Part of Work Less, Make More is experimenting, and you have to try new things to see what works best for you. A healthy relationship with failure means you're willing to try something new and not be perfect at it. As one of my clients said so eloquently, "We all want to have a daughter who plays the piano. We just don't want to listen to the wrong notes." Learn to love the wrong notes because they're an indication that you're learning something new.

The wrong notes are the pathway to becoming a master. How can you become a master if you're unable to make a mistake? You can't. It's okay to make mistakes; it's not okay to beat yourself up because you didn't do it perfectly.

Make a Mistake on Purpose

When my clients face their perfectionism blocks, I request that they make a deliberate mistake every day for seven days. Something small, but something that isn't perfect. Like sending out a memo with a typo. Showing up for a meeting five minutes late. Not returning a phone call within 24 hours. Will your life end if you make one little mistake? No. Yet it'll teach you how to live a life of excellence, not perfection.

If you're courageous, I challenge you to go to work tomorrow with mismatched socks. Put a blue sock on one foot and one black sock on the other. Yes, I know, you won't match. You'll be imperfect. Don't tell anyone what you have done, and see who notices.

Give Yourself Little Gifts of Generosity

The single best way for you to bring more joy into your life is to practice random acts of generosity. Start by being kind to yourself. Write yourself a thank-you letter and mail it. Send yourself flowers. Buy a nice gift for yourself *for no reason at all*. Don't share with anyone what you're doing, because it's your own little secret. Learn how to appreciate who you are without tying your feelings to your performance.

Pay close attention to what part of your life you're putting on hold because you haven't lived up to your own perfect standards. Isn't it time to move beyond how you're currently living?

Handling the time machine is about taking back control. It's about noticing how you're stopping yourself from moving ahead and blasting through those old behaviors. Having a handle on the time machine is not about learning some fancy time management system. It's as easy as deciding what you want your life to be about and making sure you invest the time in the activities that will get you there. I know you can do it.

Exercises

1. Take out your journal and finish this sentence 20 times: If I didn't have to do it perfectly, I would . . .

2. What do you want to do on your Free Days? Take out your journal and come up with 100 things you want to do on your Free Days. Then schedule at least one activity to do this weekend.

3. What do you want to do on your Support Days? That's probably a pretty good question. Pull out your calendar and schedule in at least two Support Days every week for the next month. Stick to your plan and do Support activities only on those days.

4. What do you want to do on your Laser Days? Develop a step-by-step plan of what you're going to do on your next four Laser Days. Most people struggle with how to fill their time with Laser activities, so take the time now to plan where you're focusing your attention. Pull out your calendar and schedule in at least one Laser Day every week for the next month. Stick to your plan and do only Laser activities on those days.

5. If you're a big procrastinator, ask yourself: "How does it serve me to keep putting my life on hold?" Open your journal and write for three pages as you reflect on this question. What shows up that gives you an insight about what frightens you?

6. Spend some time in your journal describing what your day looks like when its tempo is sped up, rushed, full of adrenaline. How do you feel, going through this hectic day?

Then compare it to a day with a slower tempo. What's different about how you feel on a calm day?

7. Identify what's on your plate. Delegate the items you can. Then pull out your calendar and schedule in the remaining activities. No, you don't have to complete them all this week. Give yourself time to get them done, but get them on your schedule today.

CHAPTER 5

Say Yes to Yourself

No matter how busy you are, many of you still dutifully take on more and more and more: attending cocktail parties because a client invited you, working at bake sales at school, leading a new project team even though you have no interest in it, helping out a friend on a business venture. It's especially hard for you to say no when someone tells you two things: "You're perfect for this because you're so good at . . ." or "If you don't do it, it won't get done."

Learning to say no is vital to your success in Work Less, Make More. One of the biggest blocks you may have is wanting to please other people before you please yourself. Think about that. The reason you say yes is often because you don't want someone else to think badly of you. Somehow it's okay for you to feel bad about yourself.

It's not okay anymore.

One of my clients has a very difficult time saying no. Amy is the type of person you want as your friend. When you're feeling down, Amy will send you flowers, mail you a get-well card, or e-mail over a funny note. She's always saying, "Please let me help you. I want to help you." Her warmth and love are felt by everyone who comes in contact with her.

While all this seems honorable, Amy had a big challenge. She spent so much of her time helping everyone else, she didn't have the energy to work on her own business. A creative genius, Amy is a phenomenal graphic designer. She desperately wanted to create a business that allowed her to use her talents, but she found herself always caught up in her friends' activities. Right when Amy was in the middle of a project, her phone rang. Someone was calling for a favor, so she dropped everything and rushed to that person's aid. This didn't happen every once in a while; it happened all the time.

If you need a ride to the airport, call Amy. If you need some technical help with your computer, call Amy. If you just need someone to talk to, call Amy. Amy found herself never having the time to find new business, eat properly, exercise, or work on current projects. The only time she had to herself was between 11 P.M. and 2 A.M., right before she fell asleep at her computer.

Saying no starts with saying yes to yourself first. What I suggested to Amy was she needed to put herself first, not her family or friends, her company or career, her possessions or accomplishments. Just herself first. Amy needed to learn in order for her to share her caring warmth with everyone else. She needed to learn to say yes to herself.

Okay, okay, so you're already arguing with me. You think it's selfish to think of yourself first. That's exactly what Amy said. "Jen, I believe that in order to make a difference in this world, I need to help other people." I believe that, too. The only problem is unless you put yourself first, you will not have the passion, the brilliance, or the ability to take care of anyone else. Period. End of story.

Think about it this way. Your life is like a beautiful, golden cup. It sparkles in the sun, glistens with its beauty. (Your life is like that, you know.) Every time you give to someone else, you reach inside your cup and take something out. Someone asks, you reach in and give. Someone else asks, you reach in again. And again. And again.

But if you don't take time to replenish who you are, if you

don't take time to take care of you, you never fill up your cup. Then one day you reach in to take something out, and there's nothing left to give. But you give anyway. That's what you're supposed to do, after all. You keep giving when you have nothing left to give, so you become resentful and frustrated. You feel exhausted, yet you're still asked to give. And you want to keep giving. Yet you failed to fill your cup back up. The only way to fill yourself up is to say yes to yourself first.

Rather than spend all your time taking care of everyone else, take care of yourself as a gift to everyone else and expect them to take care of themselves as a gift to you. Your gift to the world is being the best you can be. In return, you can share who you are with all the world.

Look at your life right now. You're stressed out. Burned out. You're taking care of everyone else, and you're at a critical place in your own life. If you stay on the path you're on, you won't have enough strength to do anything for anyone else. Learn how to take care of yourself by saying no to those things that don't matter, and you'll find yourself giving more and more to everyone else, without hurting yourself in the process.

The next step on the Work Less, Make More journey is learning how to say yes to yourself. Taking care of yourself—extremely good care of yourself—goes a long way in helping you get to where you want to go.

Now don't tell me you don't have the time to take great care of yourself. We've spent the past four chapters cleaning out your life so you have the time. If you still don't have the time, go back and start this book over. You cannot add more things to your life— what the next part of this book is all about—until you make space for them. If you keep adding and adding, you'll end up in a worse place than you already are.

HOW TO SAY YES TO YOURSELF

It's a sad fact that no one taught you how to nurture yourself. You learned how to take care of your lawn, your car, and your Mont

Blanc pen, but taking care of yourself probably wasn't part of your training.

Many of you are thinking: "How hard can it be to take better care of myself?" It may seem like an easy thing to do, but it's not. Look at Amy, the client I told you about before. It would seem logical to take the time to eat properly, sleep enough, exercise, meditate, and have free time. It is logical, but that doesn't mean it happens.

Look at your routine when you first get up in the morning. Most people set the alarm for the last possible second. They jump out of bed and rush through the house getting themselves—and their families—ready. They speed through getting showered and dressed. They eat breakfast in the car or they skip it altogether. Rushing is what I call bad self-care.

As they go through the day, it may get worse. Many people work through lunch or grab a sandwich from the vending machine. They jam their schedules so full they don't even have time to use the restroom. Then they bring their work home and fall asleep. Perhaps they turn on the TV during dinner—or work through it. Does your day sound much different?

Where in that day do most people stop to take care of themselves? That's exactly my point. You say yes to your family, your schedule, your colleagues, your customers, and you forget to say yes to yourself.

What can you do throughout your day to make your experience more enjoyable? Saying yes to yourself means treating yourself as if you were the precious gift you are. A few ideas on how to take better care of yourself are on the opposite page.

When you focus on yourself, it's amazing what happens. Your dreams begin to unfold, and you are no longer blocking your own success. Suddenly, you'll start doing what's necessary to work less and make more. Funny, but it'll seem as if it happened overnight.

Pull out your journal and start developing an action plan to take better care of yourself. What are some simple things you can add to your life in order to say yes to yourself?

How to Take Better Care of You

- Get a massage.

- Stop at your favorite coffee shop for a leisurely cup of decaf coffee.

- Get up 30 minutes earlier so you don't have to rush.

- Get to bed 30 minutes earlier so you feel refreshed.

- Take time to eat a nourishing breakfast.

- Develop a 30-minute exercise routine you do every day.

- Meditate for 10 minutes before you get up.

- Pray before you rise to bless the coming day.

- Write for 20 minutes in your journal.

- Read 10 pages of a great book.

- Cuddle with your spouse or your children before you go to sleep.

- Make yourself breakfast in bed.

- Buy fresh flowers so you awaken to the beautiful smells.

- Bake bread for a warm feeling in your home.

- Have your lunch outside—alone.

- Go for a 20-minute walk to clear your head.

- Eat your meals sitting down at a table and enjoy the flavors.

- Turn off the TV and tune into yourself instead.

SAYING NO TO OTHER PEOPLE

Part of saying yes to yourself may mean saying no to something—or someone—else. It's up to you to determine what's most important in your life. You've done a great job in defining what's most important, in the first four sections of Work Less, Make More, and now it's time to make sure you *live* what's most important.

Saying no is hard. I know; I've had a very tough time with it. When I was six months into launching my coaching company, I had this great idea to start an innovative virtual company. I was excited, and I called a friend to share my idea. He got excited, too, and we decided to start the business venture together. Within our first three months, we were profitable. Anyone who's owned a business understands what a feat that was—and is. The potential of this new, virtual business was tremendous, yet after just a few months into it, I realized my heart wasn't invested in the idea.

While working on the virtual business, I was also actively building my coaching company. I found myself annoyed with all the work the other business took because it diverted my attention away from coaching. I started snapping at my partner, and then I'd find myself apologizing—all in the same breath. Time after time, I thought about quitting the virtual business, but one thought kept coming into my mind: the money. How could I in good conscience walk away from something with that much potential?

I remember sitting in my office with tears in my eyes one afternoon because my heart was telling me to give up the virtual business. My love and my passion were focused on coaching, not on being some big-shot cofounder of a virtual company. I knew I had to say no. I had to say no to my partner, to the opportunity, and to the potential of making a lot of money in that business. Let me tell you, that was one of the hardest no's I've ever had to say.

It's uncomfortable when you're first learning how to say no. Just as when you were learning how to ride a bike, you may get some skinned knees and a few bruises. The key is to keep saying no because you'll soon have the skill down pat.

The first step in learning how to say no is determining what pushes your buttons. What always gets you to say yes? For example: "But you're so good at it." "You have to help me. If you don't, no one will." "You have to help. You're my only answer." What are the five things that get you to say yes? Once you know what triggers you to say yes even when you want to say no, then you can move into action: actually saying no.

An important thing to remember is that it's crucial that you tell the truth when you say no. If you lie about something, you'll always get caught. For example, you may tell friends you can't go with them somewhere, and then they see you out at the mall with someone else. It's awkward and dishonest. I'm not suggesting you learn how to become a great liar. Not at all. Learning how to say no *with integrity* requires that you tell the truth.

Here are seven ways you can say no.

Just No

Thanks, but I'll have to pass on that. Say it, then shut up. You don't want to ruin the effect.

The Gracious No

I really appreciate your asking me, but my time is already committed. This is a gentle way to say no.

The "I'm Sorry" No

I wish I could, but it's just not convenient. The real masters of the "I'm Sorry" No somehow get the other people to apologize over and over for even asking. I'm always amazed when I see this happen.

The "It's Someone Else's Decision" No

I promised my coach I wouldn't take on any more projects without discussing them with her first. This postpones the decision and allows you to decide if you really want to say no. Only use when you're not sure if you want to say yes.

The "My Family Is the Reason" No

Thank you very much for the invitation. That's the day of my son's soccer game, and I never miss those. Great reasons also include birthdays, anniversaries, high school graduations. . . . Just be sure you're not making it up. Tell the truth. You may think this is the easiest no to say, but it's not. How often have you said no to your family in order to work? My point exactly.

The "I Know Someone Else" No

I just don't have the time to help you, but let me recommend someone else I know. A great way to say no while still helping the person by giving another option. It's often easiest to say no when you can offer another solution.

The "I'm Already Booked" No

I appreciate your thinking of me, but I'm afraid I'm already booked that day. Use this one especially if you've blocked out time for yourself. It's horrible to break a date with someone else— even worse if you break the date with yourself.

Never, ever say maybe. Maybe is only a way of postponing a decision. When you know you want to say no, say no. Otherwise, you're not playing fair with yourself—or with others. And saying "maybe next time" makes it harder and harder to say no the next time. Don't fall into this trap.

One of my clients has a knack for raising money for new start-up ventures, and many of his friends understand how good he is. Jeremy and I were reviewing his priorities during one of his coaching sessions, and he told me a friend had called and asked him to help out. His friend was thinking about starting a new business, and Jeremy was the perfect guy to help with the business plan. His friend did not have the financial means to pay Jeremy for his time, and Jeremy knew that the business plan would take a minimum of 25 hours to complete. He simply didn't have the time to invest in a free project. Jeremy was heavily in debt, and he was focused on reducing his debt by increasing his income.

At any other time in his life, Jeremy could easily have helped his friend out. But not this time. Jeremy freely admitted he often says yes because he wants the other person to like him, even if that means putting himself in a jam. He said, "Jen, how can I say no to a friend? This guy really needs me to help him with his business. He says I'm the only one who can do the job. If I say no, his dream will die."

Do you think Jeremy was the only answer to his friend's dilemma? Of course not. I challenged Jeremy to say no, and as I shared with him the seven different ways to say no, he realized he had another friend who also could provide the financial analysis for his friend—and that friend owed Jeremy a favor. Jeremy was able to say no yet recommend another resource to help his friend out at the same time.

Saying no to other people means staying true to who you are. You won't work less and make more if you're not able to distinguish between saying yes because you want to say yes and saying yes because you're afraid to say no.

SAYING NO TO CLUTTER

Another huge part of your life may need a big no. It's called clutter. One of the biggest reasons many of you aren't more productive is you're drowning in a sea of paper. Junk mail. Memos. Budgets. Post-it notes.

Not only does clutter cost you time—you're constantly wasting time searching for things—but it costs you energy. Every time you walk into your office, you use energy being annoyed at yourself. The head trash starts in. *I should be more organized. I need to take the time to clean up in here. I just can't find a thing.* That negativity takes energy away from your brilliance at work. No wonder you feel like you're on a treadmill going nowhere.

One of my clients has a real issue with clutter. Being disorganized consumes her life. When Martha walks in the front door of her home, the first thought in her mind is, *This house is a mess.* She then frets about all the clutter that is piling up in drawers, closets, and on tables. Her office looks the same way. Stacks and stacks of paper that Martha says she'll someday get to. Instead, the stacks serve as a way for her to tell herself how disorganized she is. Martha spends countless hours talking about her clutter rather than doing anything about it. Her reason for not handling the mess? She's too busy.

The real definition of *clutter* is postponed decisions. One of the reasons Martha doesn't handle the clutter in her life is because doing so would force her to make some hard decisions. Think about the stack of paper on your desk. You get a memo or a letter that you need to respond to, but you're not quite sure what to say. Instead of making the decision, you stick it on top of the pile of other postponed decisions. All those decisions just sit there until you're forced to make a decision. And usually that push comes from someone else.

If you want to start working less and making more, it's time to start making decisions. This program is about taking responsibility for your life and getting your life back on track. Clutter gets in your way, and it's time to say no.

The first step in overcoming the clutter in your life is cleaning up the mess. I call it cleaning up neglect. Here are a few ideas on how to get started.

Start with Something Small

Many times you know you need to bite the bullet and throw away the majority of the stuff that's cluttering up your life. Yet when you look around, you realize the task is just too big to handle, so you ignore the problem. Rather than forcing yourself to declutter everything at once, start with something small. Leave your office alone and start with the car. Or decide you want to declutter the junk drawer rather than your closets. Perhaps you want to start by cleaning out one file a day. Take something that seems manageable and start there.

Use the Momentum of the Small Stuff to Get You Going

You'll find that the energy you use to declutter your car may propel you into tackling bigger tasks. Grab a bunch of trash bags or the recycling bin and start throwing stuff away. The key to remember is that you're not reorganizing the piles; you're discarding what you no longer need. There's a big difference. Reorganizing your piles is still postponing a decision. Instead, throw stuff away. If you get rid of it, you no longer have to organize it.

Keep asking yourself an important question: "What is the worst possible thing that could happen to me if I did not have this?" If you can live with the consequences, get rid of it. Be ruthless with the clutter in your life.

Box Up the Clutter

Martha developed a system that allowed her to get instant gratification from decluttering on a limited schedule. Rather than taking hundreds of hours to reorganize, Martha went through her home and office and put all the clutter into boxes. In a short time, she could actually see the top of her desk. Her task was to go through one box a week at home and at the office and sort through whatever was in there. She got immediate satisfaction from cleaning up without investing hundreds of hours, and she took baby steps to prevent herself from being overwhelmed at the decluttering task.

Ask for Help

It's much easier to declutter your office if you ask someone to help you. Ask your most organized friend to spend the day with you at the office helping you clean up the neglect in your life. Perhaps there's someone at the office who is always giving you suggestions on how to clean up. This is the perfect candidate to help you.

If you're serious about decluttering once and for all, one of the best ways to get a handle on clutter is to hire a personal organizer, a professional who gets paid to organize your life. Personal organizers will come into your office and help you get back on track. It's funny, but if you pay someone to help you, chances are pretty good you'll succeed in decluttering your life.

Spend One Hour a Week Cleaning Things Up

Oftentimes the reason you don't rid yourself of clutter is because you simply get overwhelmed with all the stuff you need to sort through. First, I want you to buckle down and spend one full day cleaning up your mess in your office. Start at work; it's much easier than it is at home.

Logic would tell us to focus on keeping things clean by spending 10 minutes a day. Many of my more creative clients (myself included) cannot get themselves into the habit of spending 10 minutes a day organizing the day's mess. It just seems too disciplined or doesn't fall into your natural way of doing things. Instead, let the mess pile up each week, and spend one hour every single Friday for the rest of your life decluttering. Every Friday. Every week.

It allows you to walk into your office on Monday with a clean desk and a clear conscience. And it allows you to be as messy as you want throughout the week without feeling guilty. Just use one hour on Fridays making your office immaculate before the coming week. It works.

The trick to successful decluttering is keeping your life that way. Once you've cleaned up your office, there's a simple system you can use to stay focused and clutter free. It's called Do It, Delegate It, or Dump It.

Do It

That means you do it now and don't handle the paperwork a second time. It also means the pile on your desk does not exist. It's done. You've handled whatever it was that you needed to handle. Suck it up and just do it.

Delegate It

That requires that you ask yourself, "Who can help complete this project or task so I can stay focused on my most important activities?" Go back to Chapter 3, Harness the Power of Focus, for more information on successful delegating.

Dump It

That is very simple. Dump as much as possible into the trash can the first time you touch it. Most of the stuff on your desk can be thrown away or recycled. So many times you have files full of stuff you thought you just might use again sometime. How many times do you really dig through old files? Hardly ever. When I was in corporate America, I used to say, "If it's that important, I'm sure someone else kept a copy."

The key is to use this system with everything. It allows you to make one of three decisions on everything that comes into your life. No more postponed decisions for you.

If you find yourself with piles all around you, don't waste your energy being annoyed. It's time to say no to clutter.

SAYING NO TO INFORMATION OVERLOAD

We live in the communications age. I'm in awe every day of the new products, new services, and new stuff that are invented to help us communicate faster and faster with each other. Computers, e-mail, fax machines, cellular phones, pagers . . . they allow us to get in touch with anyone any time, any place, anywhere.

That's precisely the problem. Please, don't get me wrong. Technology is a vital piece of helping you work less and make more, especially if you're focused on saving time. Microwaves save you time at dinner. Fax machines demand immediate responses. E-mail allows you to respond in the middle of the night if

131

you want to. The Internet keeps you from spending the whole afternoon at the library.

There's just one problem. All this new technology allows other people to reach you any time, any place, anywhere. Just the other day I was in my office and a fax landed on my desk. I had barely glanced at it when the phone rang and a client I was working with asked me what I thought about the material. He actually expected me to give him an answer right then. In days past, we used to be able to think things over. It took time for the postal carrier to deliver our items, sometimes three to four days. We could always buy ourselves some time.

That's not the case anymore. Face it. We live in a sped-up, I-wanted-it-yesterday world. Add to that problem that we are bombarded with information every single day. Our fax is always ringing. We need to respond to 50 or more voice mails every day. Our e-mailboxes are overflowing. All this technology is demanding more of our time when we just don't have the time to give.

How do you manage the information overload? Here are a few ideas.

Take Responsibility for the Information You Consume

You can easily overdose on information that bombards you every day. You get overwhelmed or desensitized, so you stop paying attention. You stop learning, and your life suffers because of it.

A great way to handle the flow is to go on an information diet. Eliminate all the worthless stuff that blasts at you every day. You know, the stuff that doesn't help you become more successful—TV and newspapers for example—and focus on information that inspires you. Yes, I'm suggesting that you spend a week not watching television or reading the newspaper. My husband and I stopped watching the news two years ago. If anything "big" happens that we need to know about, like when Princess Diana or Mother Teresa died, someone always tells us.

My father-in-law loves to call and fill us in on the world news. I have never known anyone—except news anchors, reporters, and producers—who became more successful because they watched TV. Turn it off.

There are other ways to control the amount of information you consume. Give away books that don't serve you anymore. Throw out the junk mail without opening it. Delete useless e-mail. Call companies that send you e-mail and ask to be taken off their lists. I have a client who copies a "please take me off your list" letter and e-mails or mails it out to every company that sends her junk mail. She has dramatically reduced the amount of mail and e-mail she receives. The key to working less and making more is taking back control of what you put into your brain.

Handle E-mail Overload

Although I believe e-mail is the most innovative product ever developed, it has also become a big user of our time. One of my past clients had a real problem with e-mail. She had a function on her computer that buzzed every time a new e-mail arrived in her box. She would immediately turn to her computer and read the e-mail. She once called it an addiction. As you can imagine, her productivity was horrible because she spent so much time responding to unimportant e-mail.

For those of you who hear a bell every time you receive a new e-mail, turn that function off. If you don't know how to do that, get out your computer manual and figure it out. You do not need to check every single e-mail the minute it arrives.

Instead, check your e-mail once or twice a day at the same time and stick to it. I average more than 80 e-mails a day, and I check my box twice a day—once when I arrive at my office and again right before I leave for the day. I let people know that I check my box twice a day. That way they don't expect a 30 minute turnaround. Communicate how you're handling e-mail, and you'll find people will adjust to your schedule. Saying no is learning how to take back control.

Control the Telephone

Just as the phone is an incredible tool to allow you to reach some-one in seconds, it also allows other people to reach you in seconds. The telephone was one of the most disruptive inventions ever cre-ated until cellular phones came out on the market. I used to work for a cellular company, and I found myself never getting any work done because that little phone was always ringing. There's some-thing about a ringing cellular phone that made me want to answer the call—even if I was in the middle of a conversation with some-one else. Every time that phone rang, I felt prestigious about being "so important" that I had to answer every cellular call that came in. When I look back on it today, I realize that I linked being successful with being busy. A way to prove I was busy was to delude myself into thinking I had to be accessible at all hours of the day. Truth was, nine times out of ten, the call could have waited.

Make sure you use the telephone for *your* convenience. If you have a personal assistant, have that person screen calls for you. Ask your assistant to take a message when you're in the middle of important activities. You lose momentum every time you answer the phone right when you're concentrating on something impor-tant. Why hinder your success when you can control it?

You can also do the same thing you do with e-mail: Answer and return phone calls at specific times during the day. It is not necessary to pick up the phone every time it rings.

Take Control of Your Faxes and Mail

The same strategy applies to faxes and mail. Develop a routine at the same time every day when you sort through mail and reply to faxes. Be sure to use the Do It, Delegate It, or Dump It philoso-phy when looking at your mail.

Learn to Speed Read

When I was a kid, I learned how to speed read. This is the single most valuable skill I ever learned. It allows me to speed through

200-page books in an hour, and it gives me the ability to read a document in half the time it takes the average person. I save hundreds of hours a year by reading fast. Most important, I hardly ever feel as if I'm overloaded with information. I can read quickly and take what I most need. Invest your time in learning this skill, too.

Those who are successful in handling information overload all do one thing: They take responsibility for controlling the flow. Don't allow others to bombard you with information. You decide when and where you'll sort through the information. This is your life, not theirs.

LEARNING HOW TO SAY NO TO OLD HABITS

One of the reasons you don't Work Less, Make More is because you just can't get rid of your bad habits. The stuff that doesn't serve you anymore. No matter how hard you try, you just can't break these bad habits.

The reality is that what you do and what you think determine what you get in the world. Yes, what you do and what you think. The stuff that happens automatically without your thinking about it. Left untouched, the past will create the future. That means your habits will create your future. For our good habits, that's a good thing. A darn good thing. For our bad habits, watch out.

What habits are stopping you from having the success you want?

The first step is identifying the habits that keep getting in your way. Become aware of what's happening automatically. Make a list of five habits that prevent you from being more successful. For example:

- Procrastination. (Always waiting until the last minute to do really important stuff.)
- Smoking. (You take too many breaks to smoke rather than work.)
- Interrupting people. (Yeah, that can become a habit, too.)

I bet you can come up with at least five habits that hold you back.

The trick is to tell the truth. If you're not sure what habits are holding you back, ask someone. It's amazing how easy it is for someone else to see the habits that we're demonstrating. Now's the time to get down to the truth.

The five habits that hold you back are:

1.

2.

3.

4.

5.

The biggest mistake most people make is they focus all their attention on breaking their bad habits. They get up one morning and say, "Today, I'm going to quit smoking." By noon, they're smoking again. It's not because they don't have willpower. It's not because they are lazy or big, fat failures. It's because they think that just deciding to give it up is enough.

It just doesn't work that way. The bad news is you've spent years developing those habits. You won't be able to break them easily. At least not if you push and struggle to get rid of them. Putting your attention on something makes it even stronger, so if you put all your attention on breaking a habit, you only make its hold on your life more powerful.

The answer to breaking old habits is developing alternatives. If you don't have another option than smoking, you're going to smoke. It's that simple. You need an alternative. Why do you think so many people who stop smoking gain weight? It's because they traded smoking for overeating. They found an alternative—although still unhealthy—to smoking.

How do you break old habits? You find alternatives, and you

implement some good, old-fashioned discipline. It means you work little by little, step by step to implement an alternative into your life. The old cliche "It takes 21 days to make a habit" is true. I actually think it takes more than 21 days, but at least you're on the path to developing a new habit in your life.

Go back to the list you made of the five habits that prevent your success. Come up with at least three alternatives to replace each old habit. That way you can choose the one alternative—or a combination of them—that works best for you.

Now pick one alternative from your list of 15 that you want to develop into a new habit. What do you need to do every day to make this a habit? Start right now. No matter what, start right now.

I'm sure many of you can appreciate this real-life example on starting a new habit. It has to do with exercise—the one habit lots of people have problems developing.

When I was single and working in my first job after college, I had a lot of time on my hands. An important thing in my life was exercise, so I worked out five days a week in a tough aerobics class. I even started teaching step aerobics three to four times a week.

By the time I got married, I was fit. I looked good. About 10 months later, my husband and I moved to a new city. I didn't join a gym right away, and I didn't continue teaching aerobics. Guess what? I woke up four years later and realized that my fit, healthy body had left me. I was overweight. Unfit. Fat.

The reason this happened was I got out of the habit of working out. I broke my discipline of working out five days a week. And four years later, I was fat. For two years, I tried to push myself to work out again. No success. I put all my attention into trying to stop eating the foods I wanted to eat that weren't necessarily healthy choices. That concentration of power helped me to eat even more of those foods.

When I thought about developing the habit of exercising again, I would get excited. For the first few days, I would rush off to the gym energized about my new lifestyle. But when it starting feeling *uncomfortable,* when my mind would tell me over and over again that I really wanted to stay home instead of getting dressed for the gym, I listened. And I stopped working out.

The day my exercise program turned around was the day I realized that feeling uncomfortable was part of the process. I needed to feel uncomfortable for a while because I was developing a new habit. Feeling uncomfortable is not always fun, but it's part of the process. In my heart, I wanted to develop the habit of exercising more than ever—and not just because I missed my body. Exercise has always been great therapy for my mind. Feeling uncomfortable for a while was part of the process, and when I finally learned that lesson, exercise became part of my life again.

Notice what I just wrote. I was ready to feel uncomfortable for a while as the new habit developed. The key to developing new habits is repeating them over and over again *plus* noticing how you're feeling. It's important to appreciate and honor feeling uncomfortable. Change is always uncomfortable. Embrace it. Don't run from it.

I challenge you to develop a list of the 12 habits you want to create during the next year. What are the things, that if you did them every day, would help you create an incredible future?

The mistake most people make is they try to create more than one new habit every month. Don't do it. It's hard enough to create one more habit at a time. Go back through your list and write down what month you want to implement this habit. Remember it takes 21 days to develop a new habit. You have at least 30 days each month to make your new behavior a permanent part of your life.

Start off the beginning of each month with a new habit. Focus all your attention on that one habit and make it a part of your routine. Remember, left untouched, your habits determine your future. Will your current habits create the future you want?

SAYING NO WHEN YOU SAY YES

There's an important thing you need to know as you continue to work toward working less and making more. Saying no is a skill

---

Habits You Can Develop

• Connecting with one person I really care about every day

• Drinking eight glasses of water every day

• Writing one thank-you note every day

• Making 10 new business calls every day

• Reading 10 pages of an inspiring book every day

• Writing three pages in my journal every day

• Taking a leisurely walk alone for 10 minutes every day

• Spending 30 minutes every day doing nothing

• Working up a sweat for 45 minutes every day

• Ironing my clothes the night before so I don't rush around in the morning

• Getting up at 6 A.M.

• Connecting with at least one current customer every day to express thanks for his or her business

What are the 12 habits you want to develop?

---

you'll need to use every single day. So far in this book, we've been focused on cleaning out the old and bringing in the new.

Once you get your life focused in a way that works for you, you need to apply a very important skill: saying no to something before you say yes to something else. Whenever you say yes, you must say no to something else.

Let me give you an example. You find yourself at a dinner with some friends, and you're introduced to a wonderful, inspiring entrepreneur. The two of you strike up an interesting conversation about his new business venture. Turns out it's exactly the type of project you could get excited about. The chemistry between you is great, and he asks you to invest 40 hours in helping him develop his business plan. His needs fit your skills perfectly, and you want to say yes right on the spot. Do you?

Most people would make the mistake of saying yes and move forward with the project without shifting their priorities. In about two weeks, they'd find themselves overwhelmed with everything that's going on in their lives. They forgot to say no to something in order to say yes to this new opportunity.

Before you say yes and invest your time, what are you going to say no to? I understand saying no may be short term, but you still have to take something off your plate before you add anything new. By all means, go for the new opportunity if it makes your heart sing. Just know you need to choose what you won't be spending your time on.

Learning how to say no whenever you say yes will keep you working less to free you up to make more.

Exercises

1. Pull out your journal and make a list of 25 ways you can take extremely good care of yourself. If you're already doing a pretty good job, take it to the next level. Create a life of simple luxuries.

2. Pick out five things from the list you just made and implement them immediately into your life. Turn these activities into your daily self-care routine.

3. Say no 50 times this week. That's not 20 times, not 30 times—it's 50 times. (Saying no to your kids or your dog doesn't count. That's too easy!) Practice all seven techniques and see which one feels the most comfortable for you.

4. One of the best ways to clear out some space in your life is to get rid of all the old things in your life that no longer serve you. Go into your closet and donate all your old clothes to your local shelter. Give away everything that's out of style or doesn't fit and the items you don't like anymore.

5. Tackle that stack in your office this week by using the Do It, Delegate It, or Dump It technique. Keep doing, delegating, and dumping until that stack is gone.

6. Develop your 12-month new habit plan. Which habit do you want to start this month? What about next month and the next month? Prioritize when you'll be implementing each habit and get started on what you want to do this month.

7. What things do people ask you to do that you don't enjoy or like doing? Don't procrastinate about them. Make a list of people you know who you can refer this work to. If you don't know anyone, make the effort to create a relationship with someone who would love to do this work.

AUTHOR'S NOTE

You have just completed Part I of this book. At this point, you now have the tools to clear out time and space in your life in order to focus on the main reason you bought this book: to make more. I like to call the first part of the book "cleaning up neglect." You spent a large amount of time getting rid of beliefs, behaviors, relationships, and habits that no longer serve you. It's as if you've created a big gap in your life that's ready to be filled in with new possibilities. You should be in a place where you can maximize making more.

When you read about making more, I want you to think not just about making more money, but also about making more of your life. This next part of your journey is to design the life you want to live. I've focused on giving you the tools you need to put your creative power to work. That's what redesigning your life is all about. Deciding what you want, then creating a way to make it a reality. This part of Work Less, Make More is exhilarating. Exciting. Inspiring.

Next page—let's get back to work.

Part II
MAKE MORE

The single best way to create high income is to understand that money means freedom, especially when you're focused on Work Less, Make More. The choices you'll make when you're going for freedom are much different from the choices you'll make if you're going for image. Making More is about freeing yourself from ever worrying about money again.

CHAPTER 6

Duplicate Yourself

Have you heard of Dolly? She is an exact duplication of another sheep. A clone. When the news reports about Dolly first came out, I had more than one client say to me, "Jen, I wish I could figure out a way to clone myself."

Until science comes up with a way to clone humans, we'll have to find another way. It's called *duplication*. Duplicating yourself is possible. Being able to work less comes down to finding the right people to delegate to. Being able to make more comes down to doubling, tripling, quadrupling your output without your personally spending any more time. In a word, duplication.

Duplication brings the work less make more concept to a new level. This strategy allows you to take a three-month sabbatical, and when you come home, your income has increased. Yes, increased. Isn't that what making more is all about?

Before you start developing a plan to duplicate yourself, I need to dissolve some of your fears. I know some of you are thinking, "Yeah, right. I could never find someone just like me." You're right. Most people believe duplication means finding the one perfect person who is the exact replica of you. Like Dolly, who's an exact replica of another sheep. No wonder you're feeling a bit uneasy right now. How can you put your business or career into one person's hands? That's not what duplication is. Not at all.

To work less and make more, you need to duplicate yourself *more than once*. It may take 10 other people to fill your shoes. That's okay. In fact, I prefer that you find 10 people to duplicate parts of what you do. That way if one person leaves, your whole world doesn't crash. Duplicating yourself more than once may mean upgrading your technology so you can show up in more places than just one. It may mean repackaging what you offer so you can give something similar but different to a wide variety of audiences. It may be finding a staff of people who can do what you do in some area of your business—and maybe even add a new twist or dimension.

Duplication is not about delegating. We covered that in earlier chapters. Delegating hinges on your finding the right person whose strengths are your weaknesses. A bookkeeper, for example, if you're horrible with numbers. An assistant if you don't have time for filing, copying, and computer work. That's different from duplicating.

What I'm talking about here is duplicating a part of who you are. Finding someone who is just as good as you are and hiring him or her. For example, if you want to double your sales, go out and hire a salesperson who shares your brilliance. Overnight you'll double your sales. Duplication is about maximizing your output without investing more time.

Will duplication help you generate more money? Absolutely, if you do it right. Will duplication help you make more of your life? Absolutely, if you do it right.

FINDING THE RIGHT PEOPLE

In order to duplicate, you must know yourself very well. You cannot just duplicate your abilities, but also parts of your personality. Most people go just for duplicating abilities, and they make a big mistake.

One of my clients, a financial planner, decided he wanted to duplicate what he did. John wanted to increase his income by doing more of the same thing, but he knew he didn't want to work any more hours. He was already a master delegator, and he knew the next step was duplicating himself.

John hired a woman who had the same abilities, but she had the exact opposite personality to his. He was loud and boisterous. She was quiet and thoughtful. He always had a great story or joke to share with his clients. She always brought lots of hard data to support a new investment recommendation. He focused on the positive in a crisis, whereas she focused on everything else that could go wrong in order to prevent it from occurring.

When he started delegating some of his responsibilities, she did a fine job. The strengths she had were his weaknesses, and the partnership worked well. Yet John knew he needed to up the ante and actually duplicate his sales process. She needed to meet with customers in the same manner he did. John wanted to say, "My schedule is jammed this week, yet my assistant is a clone of who I am. She'll be able to help you in the same way I can." Duplication at its finest.

The transition wasn't very smooth. His customers started complaining. The percentage of prospects who became paying clients dropped dramatically. John didn't understand. The duplication process should have worked.

Here's why this experiment failed. John's replacement, the woman he had handpicked, did not fill the most important need his clients had: They missed his upbeat, no-fear style. They didn't want a serious financial planner. They wanted someone just like him. John had been lulled into believing that he must always find people who had the strengths that were his weaknesses. He even lost some customers because the woman he had chosen to duplicate himself did not duplicate his personality.

When you want to delegate responsibilities to someone, find someone who has the strengths that are your weaknesses. What we're talking about here is duplication. Successful duplication occurs when you find people who share similar qualities with you. Just as important, they share your brilliance.

What are the parts of yourself you need to duplicate? Think about your personality traits and the style in which you approach things. What is it about you that you'll need to successfully duplicate? Pull out your journal and write down 10 areas you could duplicate right now.

Feeling a little stuck? In Chapter 2, Do What You Do Best, you answered a few questions that allowed you to uncover your brilliance. I'm repeating those questions here to help you focus on the parts you need to duplicate.

1. What do you do easily and naturally?
2. What do your customers pay you for?
3. What does your company pay you for?
4. What have other people said you're really good at?
5. What activities energize you?
6. What consumes you? You know, the stuff that lights your fire.
7. What do you really want to do on your days off?
8. What qualities and skills do you see in other people that you know you have?

When you think about duplicating parts of who you are, there's something else you need to know. Finding people who are similar to who you are will create conflicts. It'll create tension. Maybe even some uneasiness.

Have you ever noticed that most of the people you have conflicts with are actually reflecting a part of you? I have a client who often has conflicts with strong, direct, outwardly self-confident women. She couldn't understand why she was butting heads with some pretty powerful women until I pointed out that these women's styles were similar to hers. They were bold, courageous, and self-assured. What a wake-up call. My client didn't honor and appreciate her direct style, and she wanted to come across as more nurturing and feminine. The conflict with these women was actually a reflection of the conflict within herself.

My client's situation is not unique. There may be one or two people in your life that you always have conflicts with. Those people most likely are similar to who you are. You have the same strengths, the same type of personality, so these people tend to reflect back the parts of you that you'd rather not see. No wonder you feel tension.

A few weeks ago, I was at a cocktail party with my husband. We met a couple who had just moved to town, and the woman really liked to talk. She interrupted us, didn't pay attention to what we were saying, and was simply more interested in her own opinion than in what we had to say.

I was disturbed by her behavior. As a coach, I pride myself on identifying and noticing the strengths someone has, but this woman got on my nerves. She annoyed me, and I didn't know why. When we got into the car to leave, I leaned over to my husband and said, "Boy, that woman sure knew how to talk a lot. I can't believe how annoying it was to listen to her drone on and on."

My husband responded by saying, "She sounded like someone I used to know." Who he meant was me. It was in that moment that I realized that what I didn't like about this woman was actually something I didn't like about who I used to be. It annoyed me that I used to drone on and on, not paying attention to anyone around me. What was even more disturbing was that I hadn't accepted that who I was helped me become who I am today. A big lesson.

Duplicating yourself requires that you leave your ego behind. It forces you to look at yourself and know yourself so well that you won't feel threatened by someone who's as good as you are. Most people are so afraid of not being the only one doing something that they make a huge mistake. They try to duplicate themselves with people who aren't as good. To make duplication work, you must find people who are as good—or better—than you are.

Henry Ford, the well-known automobile giant, did this tremendously well. He went out and hired people who were better than he was. Did you get that? Better than he was. He used their strengths to build an incredibly successful automobile empire. Was he threatened by their expertise? I bet you he was from time to time, but he knew that his ultimate vision couldn't be created without them. He put aside his ego. He learned how to harness their power and make it work for everyone else involved.

The big question that usually pops into your head is this: "If they are better than I am, why are they willing to duplicate me?" That's a darned good question. Here are a few answers.

- You bring some other incredible value to their lives that helps them become even better. You provide something they can't get anywhere else. Even though they may be more talented in some areas, you still bring such a tremendous amount of who you are to the table that they just want to be near you. They want to be around you for the same reason you want to be around them.
- You're actually one step ahead of them because you understand that duplicating yourself comes down to finding people who are better than you are. So few people truly understand and can see their own brilliance. They don't trust who they are. All they'll see is how brilliant you are, not how great they are.

How do you go about finding the right people? I've outlined some areas you need to examine before you decide who will duplicate you.

Find People Who Have the Right Personality for Your Chemistry

Look for folks who share the same chemistry as you. If you're upbeat and your customers appreciate that, find someone with the same characteristics. If your customers value your meticulous attention to detail, your clone will need to have that same quality. Don't downplay the importance of working with folks who have the same chemistry as you. Go back to the list you made of the qualities you must duplicate. Use this as your guide.

Find People Who Have a Track Record

Finding perfect clones is based not only on who they are, but also on their track records. Saying you can do something is different from actually doing it. Find people who have already done what you most need. They could bring a new twist or a new idea to what you've been doing for so long.

Find People Who Are Willing to Commit to the Long Term

Developing a powerful relationship requires that you're both committed to the same vision and the same long-term plan. The last thing you want to do is train people to duplicate you, and then they jump ship. Be very clear on what you expect from them, and find a way to determine what they want. If they're only looking for a short-term fix, go out and find someone else.

Find People Who Are Coachable

A vital part of duplicating yourself effectively is training. Select folks who are coachable. They're open to looking at their performances and improving them. You'll become their coach to ensure they'll duplicate what you want duplicated. If you're not willing to coach and train people how to duplicate you, don't bother looking for the right people. Their success does depend on how much time, energy, and passion you invest in them. Duplication is not about hiring people, then dumping them into the middle of the ocean to see if they will sink or swim.

Find People Who Have the Right Attitude

Make sure when you're looking for the right people that they have a positive mental attitude. There's nothing as frustrating as working with people who don't see the positive side of things. No matter how brilliant they are, their bad attitude will wear you down. If you find the right attitude, you can usually teach the rest.

There's an important thing you also need to remember: Finding the right people takes time. Do not rush this process and settle for just anyone. Duplicating a part of who you are is serious stuff. Look hard for the right people, but know it may take some time. It took scientists years to clone Dolly. It'll take you time to find your own clone. You can't settle for second best.

DETERMINING WHAT TO DUPLICATE—AND HOW

Duplicating yourself does not mean you must hire someone to work with you. That's limited thinking. You can find the right people who will become partners, vendors, suppliers, strategic allies, independent contractors, or employees.

When you box yourself into hiring employees, there are a whole slew of issues you need to concern yourself with: salaries, taxes, vacations, benefits, employee problems, office space, office supplies, technological tools—it goes on and on. I want you to think about creating a virtual support team. A team you personally select to duplicate parts of who you are.

First, who needs to be on your support team? A few pages ago, you spent time writing down the qualities in yourself you need to duplicate. Now it's time to determine what abilities you need to duplicate. What is it that these folks will do? Look at the three most important things you do, the activities that add the most value. Within each area, a multitude of items must get done. For example, if part of what you do extremely well is connecting with customers, following up by phone, fax, and e-mail is a very important part of building that relationship. What if you could train someone or something to duplicate the follow-up process? It would happen automatically—without your doing one thing—and the customers will feel cared for because the follow-up was way beyond their expectations.

Be warned. I'm talking about duplicating the follow-up process, not delegating it. The difference is that the person/system you create duplicates exactly what you would do if you were to do it. It's not about your dictating a letter that your assistant types. In that case, you're still doing the work. Duplication means you do not do anything to generate what needs to get done. Nothing.

Let's take the follow-up process a bit further. What are some possibilities of duplicating the follow-up process?

1. The right person to follow up via phone to answer questions, give additional information, and close the sale. This could be an employee, independent contractor, or customer service rep who specializes in following up. This person has the exact same personality that you do so the customers feel as if they were talking to you.

2. An automated system that spits out customized letters, e-mail, and faxes at the appropriate times following your first appointment. You delegate the process of operating the computer to someone else, but the computer is programmed to generate the appropriate information. The system duplicates the process.

3. Hiring a salesperson to handle the contact from first visit to sale. No need to get yourself involved with every customer, as you're out selling to a whole new bunch of customers. This usually happens naturally when a business is going through the hypergrowth stage. Why wait until that happens?

There are numerous ways to duplicate yourself and what you do. You'll start to understand the duplication process when you add it to your own life. It's time for you to add some creativity and expand your thinking to find the right duplication process for you.

Let's look at the activities you want to duplicate and how exactly you'll do them. During the next week, keep a pad of paper on your desk and start jotting down what areas you could potentially duplicate. What do you do so well that no one else can do? That's the exact thing you should duplicate. I know, it seems like an impossible feat, but it is possible.

Once you know what you want to duplicate, then come up with at least three ways to duplicate that activity. Think in terms of technology and people. How can you automate the process? Who can you bring to your team to duplicate you?

The process of duplicating yourself needs to begin right now. Work with your staff, partners, and vendors so that all your responsibilities will be handled by others. You want to be able to take a vacation without worrying about what's happening back at the office.

HOW TO USE TECHNOLOGY TO DUPLICATE YOURSELF

When we feel overloaded, one of the questions to ask is: "Who can I get to help me with this?" I suggest you ask a better question: "How can I automate this so no one has to do it?"

Let me use an example. A few years ago, the founder of Coach University, Thomas Leonard, decided to start writing a number of daily e-mail newsletters. The problem was that he found himself writing for a few hours every day, 352 days a year. Writing a weekly newsletter is time consuming enough, let alone writing a daily newsletter.

Surely this is not a way to work less and make more. Thomas was astute and asked himself how he could maximize technology to duplicate the process. Rather than delegating the writing to someone else, he instead automated the process. He went on a writing frenzy and produced a whole year's worth of material. He then used technology to automate the process. Every day the computer sends out to 10,000 subscribers the newsletter Thomas wrote months ago. His subscribers get the information they need, and Thomas is able to give it to them without doing it himself. He travels, goes on vacations, and works on other projects, yet every day his subscribers hear from him. They believe that he wrote the material that day just for them—and he wants them to feel that way. What he did was duplicate the process to free up time and space in his life. His customers get what they want, and Thomas gets what he wants. That's what I call working less and making more.

In fact, I loved his idea so much I've done the same thing with a newsletter I write called *Work Less, Make More Nuggets*. Visit my web site at www.worklessmakemore.com to subscribe. It's a free e-mail newsletter that gives you a quick shot in the arm each week about how to Work Less, Make More.

What can you automate to help you save time and make more money? During the next week, keep a pad of paper on your desk and start jotting down what areas you could potentially duplicate using technology. You may want to hire a technology consultant to observe how you work. Make it the consultant's responsibility to develop new ways for you to duplicate yourself through technology.

HOW TO KNOW WHEN DUPLICATION WORKS

How do you know if you've done it right? Take a 30-day vacation. Take a holiday where you cut yourself off from the office. I know, it takes courage to trust the folks you put in place. When you get back from your sabbatical, you'll be able to see what falls apart, what doesn't get done correctly, and what is substandard work. It'll give you insights into where your duplication process works and where it doesn't.

Will you ever be free unless you can duplicate who you are? You'll never know when you are free because you've been unwilling to test the system. Knowing that the system works gives you a sense of relief when you're not working. You'll certainly make more of your life without carrying around all that guilt.

Most people don't have the courage to test their duplication system. They don't want to feel superfluous. They want to feel as if the whole world would crash around them if they weren't there. Many times I see folks deluding themselves that the world wouldn't go on without them. *If I don't do this, everything will be ruined. Those people depend on me, and I can't let them down. Are you kidding me? I'm the only one who can do this, so I'm stuck in this job forever.*

Don't hinder your ability to *Work Less, Make More* by needing to feel needed. You *want* to feel superfluous. You want to be taken out of the picture. You want to have such strong people around you that you no longer have to worry that the job's getting done.

It's the only way to free yourself up to live the life you want to live. Don't worry. You'll find more interesting, exciting things to propel yourself forward, and you'll have the space to be the creative force behind your future success. Think duplication.

Exercises

1. Sit down with your journal and describe in detail what you do extremely well. Look at your description of your brilliance. Identify the areas you could find someone—or use technology—to duplicate.

2. Seek out the person/people you need to duplicate parts of who you are. Be very specific in what you're looking to duplicate. Your chemistry and your personality are the essence of what you're duplicating. Set up at least one meeting this week to discuss duplication with a potential "clone."

3. Pull out your journal and ask yourself this question: "What parts of myself make me the most crazy?" Be clear on your weaknesses so you can identify them in other people as well. When you find the right person to duplicate a part of who you are, don't be surprised if they also duplicate the not-so-good parts. Are you prepared for that?

4. How can you use technology to duplicate a part of who you are? How can you automate your process so you can quadruple your output? This would be a great project to present to your innovation team to brainstorm.

5. Look at the list of activities you do on a daily basis. You did this list in Chapter 3, Harness the Power of Focus. Draw a line down the middle of a blank sheet of paper. Write *delegate* on the left side of the page. Write *duplicate* on the right side. Evaluate each task you do. Can you delegate this task or should you train someone to duplicate it? Don't stop until the entire list is done. You've just developed a plan—once you have the right technology and people in place—to allow yourself to take three months off without losing money. It's up to you to put the plan into action.

6. Take a long walk around your neighborhood—alone.

7. Go back to the concept of working less. What else do you have to do in order to free up time and space in your life? What are you waiting for? Put this book down and do it.

CHAPTER 7

Add Memorable Value

When I was developing my 10-point Work Less, Make More system, I resisted using the word *value*. It's such a trendy word that everyone uses it these days, yet so few people understand what *value* really means. When you come right down to it, adding *memorable* value is a vital key to working less and making more. Yet there are often times when you're giving too much value. The trick is to know when enough is enough.

Adding value means being the most valuable person to someone else's success. *The most valuable.* That means who you are, what you do, and what you deliver is more valuable than anyone else's in the marketplace. Having a higher value means you make more money. It's true across the board. The higher the quality, the more value it carries, which usually means the more it costs—and the more money you make. Customers are glad to pay the higher price because it brings more significance to their lives.

Why is it that one consultant can charge $100 per hour while another charges $500 for the same amount of time? Because the higher-paid consultant adds more value. He or she is more valuable. What the consultant has to offer is more important in the eyes of the client. It's given a higher priority, so it's worth more.

When I use the word *customer* or *client*, I want you to think of who adds to your income. If you're a business owner, your customers would include the people who buy your product or service and your employees who interact with your customers. If you work for someone else, your customers include your external customers and your internal customers. Your boss would definitely be your customer as would the boss's boss and the boss's boss's boss. Get the picture?

What does adding value have to do with Work Less, Make More? Everything. When you're adding value, your customers keep coming back, and they refer other customers to you. You can Work Less, Make More by not having to chase new customers or finding a new job. Adding memorable value makes it easy to be in business. It's what I like to call effortless. You show up being your best, giving your customers exactly what they want and need, and your work becomes natural. You're no longer fighting, scratching, and clawing your way through the day. The challenge is to know when value is enough so you don't swing the other way: adding too much value that takes away from you.

It's time to shatter your ideas that you must exchange time for money. You don't. Think in terms of exchanging value for money. Yes, this applies to you whether you work for yourself or for someone else. It's all about what importance and significance you bring to the people who pay you.

Adding value is also about making it memorable. Do your customers know the value you're giving them? Adding value doesn't do any good if it doesn't make an impression. The reason you give value is to create loyal customers—satisfied customers are not enough in today's marketplace—and to create a powerful word-of-mouth reputation.

Just as important, I want you to determine when enough is enough. I see businesses all the time giving value to their customers that in turn dramatically reduces their own value. That is not the solution to working less and making more.

WHAT VALUE DO YOU DELIVER RIGHT NOW?

First, let's look at how you fare in the value game right now. It's good to know where you are so you can develop the strategies to make you even more valuable.

If you want to increase your income, you need to increase your value. If you work for someone else, and you want to keep your job, you need to immediately increase your value. In this volatile world of corporate downsizing and layoffs, the person who brings the most value has a job at the end of the day. The person who doesn't is soon looking for a new job.

If you work for yourself and you're not adding memorable value to your customers, you, too, will be looking for new customers at the end of the day. People today are smarter, more demanding, harder to satisfy, and less loyal. The name of the game is value. If you don't give it to them, your customers will go somewhere else. Plain and simple.

What value do you bring in the marketplace? Pull out your journal and ask yourself the questions on the following page.

HOW TO ADD MORE VALUE

How do you add more value to what you're offering? I've outlined the most important things you need to consider.

Be the Best

I spent an awful lot of time on this in Chapter 2, Do What You Do Best, but I can't emphasize it enough. When you're the best at what you do, people want to work with you. When you're the best, you naturally add value, because you think in ways others don't. You look at the situation differently from everyone else, and you come up with different solutions. You give more significance to a situation because you're a master. The great thing is you don't have to worry about these value questions because you naturally give more. It's who you are.

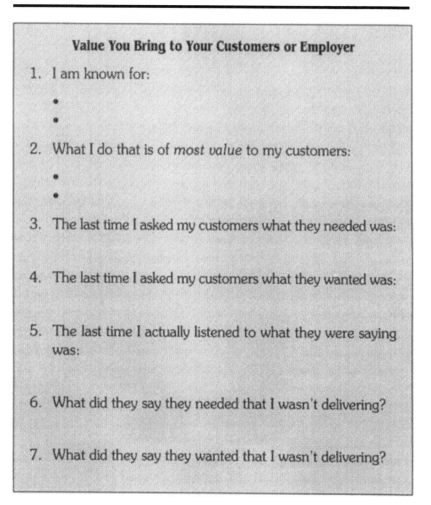

Value You Bring to Your Customers or Employer

1. I am known for:

   •

   •

2. What I do that is of *most value* to my customers:

   •

   •

3. The last time I asked my customers what they needed was:

4. The last time I asked my customers what they wanted was:

5. The last time I actually listened to what they were saying was:

6. What did they say they needed that I wasn't delivering?

7. What did they say they wanted that I wasn't delivering?

Let me give you an example. I have a friend, Jeffrey, who once shared with me his secret of success. Before I share it with you, you need to know more about Jeffrey. He is a master salesperson. An entrepreneur at heart, he owned a business that was tremendously successful because he was *that good* at sales. He sold beanbags and T-shirts, for goodness sake, and made a fortune. The thing Jeffrey did—and does—all the time is focus on being even better at sales. It's his passion. He has more than 1,000 books on sale in his library, books that he has read. More important, he applies what he's read.

Jeffrey decided one day he wanted to be a great sales trainer. So he went out and learned how to be the best. The best trainer and the best speaker. Let me tell you, he is at his best. He speaks to thousands and thousands of people every year. He stopped marketing long ago because so many people sought him out because of the value he brought.

Soon Jeffrey decided he wanted to write a column. Again, he went out and learned how to be the best possible writer. His column appears in more than 50 business publications, and he's written a few killer books on sales and customer loyalty.

Have you picked up on his secret to success? One afternoon, my husband and I were in Jeffrey's kitchen having pizza, and he shared his secret with us. He said, "My philosophy in life is this: Be the best. I decided to be a salesperson, so I became the best. I wanted to be a speaker, so I became the best. I wanted to write, so I became the best. Everything comes down to being the best, and that's how I live my life."

The great thing about Jeffrey is that he is always coming up with new and different ways to add more value to his customers. And he does it for one main reason: because he wants to stay the best. He enjoys developing new, creative ways of operating his business. And his bottom line proves that the value game is working.

A word of caution: Being the best doesn't mean you pay a tremendously high price for your success. Go back to Chapter 2, Do What You Do Best to learn how to integrate your mastery into your work. Work Less, Make More is not about giving up your life in your quest to be the best. It's about living an attitude leveraging off your mastery to work less and make more. That's why you're reading this book, isn't it?

Being the best also means being *your* best. Focusing on what you do extremely well and being at the top of your own game. Try not to get caught up in focusing on how good your competition is. If you honor your brilliance and become a master, you will blow your competition away. Don't waste your time and energy comparing yourself to them. Focus on being your very best, and success will find you.

Are you at your best?

Focus on Them, Not on You

A huge part of adding value is doing it in the way your customers want. Yes, value is about them. It's not about you.

One of my clients, Andrew, told me he was having trouble closing a big sale. He outlined the strategy he had used with the prospect, and he kept emphasizing how he couldn't understand why she didn't say yes. He said many times, "I've put so many things into the proposal. I just don't understand why she won't say yes."

I asked a simple question. "Andrew, have you asked your client exactly what she wants from you?" What do you think the answer was? He didn't know. Such an obvious thing, but so many times when you're looking at adding more value, you focus only on what you can do. You focus on the new ideas you have. The easiest way you can add more value is to ask your customers what you can do for them that you're not already doing. Listen and do exactly what they say. It's about them, not about you.

Companies mess this up all the time. The leaders of organizations waste thousands of dollars developing programs and services that the customer doesn't put any value on. The only reason the program is in place is because the president of the company thought it was a darned good idea. That's about you, not about them.

Most people treat their customers like members of some demographic or psychographic group. Creating value is to know your customers so well that you create an inseparable bond with them called the human bond. Your customers are someone's father, mother, son, or daughter. How well do you know who they are as people?

Many people make the mistake of adding value until the customer is satisfied. That's not enough today. What you need to go for is customer loyalty, and there's a big difference between a satisfied customer and a loyal customer.

Satisfied customers may say nice things about your business. Loyal customers refer all their families and friends to you. Satisfied customers are a pleasure to work with. Loyal customers feel as if they were part of your family. Satisfied customers come back when you have a big sale. Loyal customers buy even if you're not having a sale. Satisfied customers may go somewhere else if they can get a better price. Loyal customers never go anywhere else.

What do you want: satisfied customers or loyal customers? Before you answer, it's important to know that loyal customers allow you to Work Less, Make More. Why? Because it's less work to keep a loyal customer than chase a satisfied customer for repeat business, or worse, chase a prospect.

It's time to ask yourself some important questions. Pull out your journal and spend some time reflecting on these questions.

1. Why does my company really need me? What do I bring to the table that other people do not? *I want you to answer truthfully. What real value do you bring to help the company save money or make more money? If you're the owner of a company, think carefully before you answer.*

2. What do my customers pay me for? Answer this for all the customers you serve.

3. What do my customers *really* pay me for? Answer this for all the customers you serve. The answer to this question is not the product or service you deliver.

4. What do your customers need from you that you're not delivering?

5. What do your customers want from you that you're not delivering?

6. What is a problem most of your customers are having that gives you the opportunity to develop a solution for them?

7. What do your customers need from you that they haven't even told you about? Maybe they don't know it yet, but it's still your job to know. Go back to Chapter 5 and think about the problems they are experiencing.

Your assignment: Go out and talk with 10 of your customers. Tell them that you're focused on being the best and offering them incredible value, then ask them what they most need from you. You may even want to ask them the seven questions I asked you to think about.

What were the five things you learned?

1.

2.

3.

4.

5.

Solve Problems

A big mistake I often see is businesses that focus on providing benefits rather than solving problems. Your customers do not do business with you because you deliver some benefits to them. They do business with you because you solve their problems.

One of my clients works as a financial planner. We were in a coaching session when we began talking about how he works with his customers. Chris was frustrated because he required his prospects to pull all their financial documents together before they came to his office to see him. It made sense, Chris told me, because the more prepared his prospects were, the greater chance he had of making the sale. The problem was many of his prospects were procrastinating on pulling the information together because they felt a need to organize all the paperwork before they met with him. But that took time, so many prospects procrastinated on ever getting it done. They continually delayed appointments with Chris. His income was suffering because of it.

Was Chris adding value by requesting the information? No. He was adding more work to their already complicated lives. Sure, being organized before they met with Chris had merit, but he was focused on the benefits and not on solving the problems. Instead, Chris refocused his attention on solving their problems. He had his assistant set up an appointment at the customers' homes to pick up all the paperwork no matter how messy or unorganized it was. Then she organized the information and made sense of it before the clients met with Chris.

Many of Chris' prospects were simply afraid of discovering the truth about their financial situations, so he solved their problems by doing the work for them. He made it painless and effortless to do business with him. In return, Chris actually worked less and made more because he had all the information he needed in order to make the appropriate recommendations to his clients. Chris and his assistant would have spent countless hours resetting appointments, tracking incomplete financial information, and resetting more appointments. They saved time, and they closed more business at the same time.

What problem do your customers need you to solve for them?

Be a Resource

Another way to add value is to be a resource for your customers. What do I mean by *resource?* I mean you develop such a strong network that you can help your customers out with just about anything. No, not by doing it yourself—that would defeat the Power of Focus—but by connecting your customers with who they really need.

I know a phenomenal insurance salesperson. Larry is the type of guy who just warms your heart when you meet him. He's sincere. Trustworthy. Caring. The thing Larry does better than anyone else is to be a tremendous resource for his customers. Remember, he sells insurance. Yet if his customer is talking about self-publishing a book, Larry refers that person to someone he knows in the publishing industry. If a customer is feeling down, Larry often calls me looking for an inspiring quote he can share. Larry focuses on building an incredible community that he shares and refers in and out of. He has a 95 percent retention rate in his client base not only because he's a great insurance salesperson, but also because he's a tremendous resource. His clients need him.

One of the best ways to be a resource for your clients is to build your own community, your own support network of people you know and trust. Think in terms of all the resources your customers wish they had access to, and go out and build the relationships for them.

As a success coach, my team includes people in the following careers: accountants, financial planners, lawyers, business consultants, media experts, TV anchors, news reporters, bankers, spiritual gurus, other coaches, self-publishers, printers, graphic designers, web developers, writers, video producers, insurance reps, personal organizers, book agents, public relations experts, publicists, speakers, trainers, real estate agents, mortgage loan officers. . . . Are you getting the idea? In addition, I also maintain a huge library of books and Internet materials that I can give to my clients whenever they need them.

I challenge you to develop your own team. Start with 50 people. Being a resource for your customers is one of the best ways to add more value. Start here by making a list in your journal of all the types of people your customers may need. Your list may be the same as mine, but I bet it's different. Make sure it fits who your customers are and what they need.

MAKING IT MEMORABLE

Adding value is simply not enough in today's market. You have to make it memorable. Does this sound familiar? "I'm not sure why they decided not to work with us anymore. We did everything they asked and more. We often stayed late to make sure the work was done and to meet the deadlines they had imposed on us. We researched everything we could about their company, and we knew exactly what they wanted. We remembered their birthdays, sent gifts, and wrote thank-you notes. We even threw in a bunch of stuff free. I just don't understand why they went with our competition."

I'll explain it to you. The value you delivered was not what the customer wanted, and it wasn't memorable. You failed to make a lasting impression, so they found a company that would. In order to create loyal customers, you must be memorable.

In today's world, we are constantly bombarded with messages of all kinds. We're surrounded with advertising messages, voice mail messages, and e-mail messages. Many times you're so swamped with information, you fail to pay attention to what's happening around you.

Your customers have the exact problem that you do. They are as busy as you are, and many times they fail to notice what you're doing for them. That's where the "What have you done for me lately?" cliche comes from. They are guilty of forgetting the value you brought to them.

It's your job to create value that they can't help but remember. That doesn't mean you spend hundreds of dollars trying to impress them. Of course not. It means you find a way to break through the clutter and deliver memorable value.

I mention one of my clients earlier who owns a coffee shop. Dennis understands what it means to create a group of loyal customers, and he wanted to make a memorable and lasting impression on his most important customers. But how could he do it? You're thinking, yeah, how can he do it? After all, he only owns a coffee shop.

Dennis knew that his loyal customers didn't just come to his coffee shop because it was convenient for them; many of them went out of their way to frequent his location every morning. He knew they wanted to feel as if they were part of the family. His staff did what other coffee shops did. They greeted everyone with a friendly smile, called the regular customers by name, and knew what they drank. Bob wanted more. He wanted to be memorable and create a sense of connectedness among his customers.

That's why he created his Latte Wall Of Fame. His loyal customers are now rewarded by having their photos taken and posted up on the wall. Dennis added value to their experiences because he cared enough to feature them on his wall of fame. They aren't just customers, they've become his friends. Every time they walk into his store, they can't help but smile at their mug shots. The day their photos go up on the wall, they can't help but tell other people. For some of his customers, their

169

photos are the most recognition they've had all year. Talk about feeling like you're part of the family!

Notice that Dennis didn't give coffee away. He didn't lower his prices. He didn't work 100 hours a week to add more benefits for his customers. He focused on making a lasting and memorable impression. And that's exactly what he does.

WHEN IS ENOUGH, ENOUGH?

Is there a time when you're adding too much value? The answer is a resounding yes. You can add too much value, and the key is to understand when enough is enough.

Many people make the mistake of believing that adding a lot of stuff is adding more value. It isn't. After a while, the law of diminishing returns kicks in, and customers can no longer remember what's special and what's not. Worse, if you provide too much value, they may take you for granted. That means in their minds, you're not adding any value at all.

I see this all the time with consultants I know. For example, my colleague Kate has this problem. Rather than simply focusing on being a tremendous consultant, Kate is caught up in proving to the client that she is good enough.

Kate is extremely well prepared when she arrives at her clients' door, armed with an agenda of what she wants to cover. She asks brilliant questions during their time together and keeps the clients' projects on track. Yet when she leaves their offices, she feels as if her performance was not quite enough. So she bombards her clients with numerous e-mail and piles of paper—all to support whatever the client is experiencing. Kate writes an extensive newsletter that she mails quarterly, and her meeting notes are extremely detailed, so detailed that her clients typically don't even read any of the support documentation.

In Kate's mind, she's adding tremendous value by delivering much more than what the client expected. Did I mention that Kate works more than 60 hours a week? When I asked her what she's investing all her time in doing, she mentioned all the additional materials she sends her clients. Giving them all that stuff easily adds an extra 12 hours to each workweek.

Enough is enough! Kate is clearly going overboard. What the clients want is tremendous value from the time Kate spends with them. They don't want loads of stuff to clutter up their lives. Sending along a recap of the consulting meeting is an added bonus, a great way to add value. The rest of the materials are never read, so how can they be adding more value? On top of that, Kate could dramatically reduce the number of hours she's working by focusing on what the clients really need, not on providing useless information to make herself feel like she's doing a great job.

Kate believes that giving her clients more than enough information is the key to adding value. That just isn't the case. Here are some guidelines to follow to know when enough is enough.

Focus on Your Most Important Customers

When you're playing the value game, it's important to focus first on your most important customers. I often hear my clients say, "But that's not fair. If we do it for one customer, we have to do it for all of them." Says who?

Working less and making more is about playing favorites. It's about using the Power of Focus to add value where it will pay off the most. You should always divide your customer and your prospect list into your A-list and your B-list. Your A-list are the customers who add the most to your bottom line. They spend more, make repeat purchases more often, and refer more. Your A-list are your loyal customers, and they receive A-plus attention, favors, and service. You know as much about your A-list customers as you do about yourself, and they are the main reason you are in business.

Your B-list includes customers who haven't yet become loyal customers. No matter how hard you try, all your customers won't be A-list customers. You can't be all things to all people, and those who work with you occasionally go on the B-list. Those on the B-list are well cared for, but they aren't lavished with more and more value. Under no circumstances should you treat your B-list badly. Give them the best service possible. What we're talking about here is value. Invest your time, energy, and passion into adding value with your most important customers, your A-list.

Give with Joy

Another way to decide when you've given enough value is to pay attention to how you feel when you're adding value. Staying true to the Work Less, Make More concepts means you get joy from giving value, not because you want anything in return, but because you simply enjoy giving something extra.

I was in a retail store the other night. It was about 10 minutes until closing time, and I could feel the owner's dissatisfaction. I tend to ask a lot of questions when I'm shopping, and the owner grudgingly answered me. I quickly realized she was more interested in closing the store on time than she was in waiting on me. Of course, I left her store without spending a dime.

What I wanted was for her to help me enthusiastically with my purchase because she actually wanted to give me great service. Was I an A-list customer? No. But that doesn't mean I am not treated with respect. I know this business owner thought she was adding value to her customers because she was open late on Thursdays. That certainly wasn't enough for me or anyone else for that matter. Of course I wanted convenience—everyone does—but I also wanted delightful, memorable service, and I didn't get it.

Adding value is about giving because you want to give, not because you have to give.

Add Value without Degrading Who You Are

Adding memorable value is not about giving up who you are just to give the customer more value. That defeats the whole purpose of working less and making more. I get tired of hearing people say, "The customer is always right." There are times when we can't serve the customer, when it would benefit you greatly to walk away from the business.

Another key to knowing when you've crossed that line is being very clear on what products, goods, and services you provide. You can't be all things to all people, and learning how to invest your time, energy, and passion in the right customers is a big part of working less and making more. It's called *focus*. You need to know exactly who your ideal customers are before you can add more value to their lives. Do not fool yourself into believing you can provide service to everyone. You can't. Go back to what you do well and design your services around that.

The other red flag I often see is when people put their customers before themselves and their businesses. They will do anything to please the customer even if it means losing money. Now I'm not talking about losing money because your company made a mistake you needed to fix. That's called fixing a problem, not adding value. You are in business to make a profit. If you don't make a profit, you won't be in business anymore. It's as simple as that.

Take a look at Kate, the consultant I describe earlier. She was adding an extra 12 hours to her workweek to give value to her clients. I know Kate believes that her customers are more important than she is. When you look at how much time Kate invests in a client versus how much she charges that client, she loses money on almost 50 percent of her clients. That's not the way to work less and make more.

Yes, this means you're going to have to say no from time to time. In fact, just the other day I was coaching one of my clients on the idea that developing a new program for his customers would actually take too much time and money compared to the results it would bring. It was a great idea that solved a customer's problem, but the solution wasn't quite right.

When you're adding value, a rule of thumb is to add five times more value without taking any more time and money. Yes, five times more value. Kate, for example, could add five times more value without investing more time by automating her documentation process. If her clients told her they appreciated the extra value she was providing, she could hire someone to input a tremendous amount of information into her computer. The documents could be set up to go, and all Kate would need to do would be to click on the information she wanted to give her client, and then send it in an e-mail. Without automation, Kate would need to recreate her materials and invest at least one hour. With automation, the same value would take less than five minutes once the information had been entered.

Go back to the beginning of this chapter and look at what you do already to add value for your customers. How can you increase that amount by five times without adding more time or money? Brainstorm a list of at least 25 ideas in your journal.

Creating memorable value is not just about creating an impression in your customers' eyes. It's also about creating an impression in your own eyes.

Adding memorable value allows you to make more money for one simple reason: You create not only a group of not-just-satisfied customers, but also a band of loyal customers. It's your job to make sure they stay loyal without your losing sight of who you are.

Exercises

1. When could you have delivered twice as much value, but didn't? Write in your journal about what held you back. What are you discovering about who you are?

2. What do you do that's the best, and how does that tie into adding more value for your customers? Brainstorm at least 50 different ways you can enhance what you're already providing to your customers. Remember, if you work for someone else, you have customers, too.

3. Carefully evaluate what you're currently doing to add more value. Are you making the kind of impression you want to make? Ask your customers if they can tell you what value you provide. Match their definitions with the value you think you add. What did they not notice? What can you do to make it more memorable?

4. Identify the top 20 percent of your customer base, your A-list. (If you work for someone else, this A-list includes any person who can dramatically influence your career at your company.) What can you do immediately to add twice the value to what you offer them?

5. Do you know when enough is enough? What is it costing you to add value for your customers? Spend some time writing in your journal. Ask yourself this question: "Am I paying too high a price for the value I'm delivering?" Be honest with yourself and your situation.

6. Brainstorm at least 25 ways you can add five times more value without investing any more time or money. Take

your best idea and implement it. Make sure it's memorable value.

7. Get up 30 minutes early tomorrow morning. Get out your journal and write three pages before you do anything else. Write anything and everything that comes into your mind. Just get it down on paper. Don't read it over after you're done. Close your journal and get on with your day.

CHAPTER 8

Create, Innovate, and Thrive

Your ability to move to the next level of the Work Less, Make More program will be determined by your creativity. It'll be measured by your ability to come up with new solutions, develop new ideas, and deliver new services—in a way that doesn't require you to spend more time.

Think about it this way. If you think the way you've always thought and do what you have always done, you will get the results you have always gotten. I don't think that's why you're reading this book. You want to make things work better with less stress while generating more money.

No matter what challenge you face in the Work Less, Make More program, there is always a creative solution to your problem. Always. I have yet to meet a person who can't solve his or her problems with creativity.

Yet the real thing I focus on in this chapter goes beyond just being creative. It's about being innovative. *Innovation* is the economics that drives everything. That's right. Innovation allows you to make money. By itself, having great ideas won't help you generate more income, and neither will great inventions. Only innovation will because it uses both creativity and invention.

Innovation is a crucial key to working less and making more for one good reason: *It's the raw material for the creation of wealth.* Everything else is just reshuffling and redistributing what you already have. Without innovation, there isn't anything new. Nothing better or different. No new twists or new ways to package something.

Making more is much easier if you're innovative. It's what I call the path of least resistance. In today's marketplace, it's almost a requirement that you develop new and better ways of operating— all the time. Your customers are more demanding than they used to be, and you have to keep up with their demands. If you fail to innovate, your competitors will take away your customers. Your profits will dwindle because you failed to keep up. If you refuse to look at new ways of operating, you'll be left in the dust.

Look at the vinyl-record industry. One day it was king of the hill, selling millions of vinyl records every year. Until the tape deck came out, and soon thereafter, compact discs hit the streets. What happened to your vinyl record company if you didn't innovate? You were dead. Out of business. Gone.

Innovation also plays a key role in personally feeling fulfilled. Creative potential is human nature. I bet if I asked if you were creative, most of you reading this would say no. You believe that creative acts must result in something artistic, like a book, a painting, a sheet of music. That's simply not true. You are creative. We all are.

What's missing for most of you is that you long to be more creative in your work and in your life. Without creativity, the juice of innovation, your soul dies. You don't believe me? Think back to a time when you dreaded getting out of bed every day. Remember what it felt like to live your life without passion, without that creative spark. (Maybe you're there right now.) Your soul was dead. Maybe for a short time, but it was dead. It came back to life when you found something to be passionate about. Maybe it was a new job. A new relationship. A new boss. A new attitude. Something changed that made you come alive. That change had something to do with creativity. That's what I mean when I say your soul dies without creativity.

Do you remember what it feels like when you solve a problem with an idea that just came to you? That's creativity. And it's the foundation of all innovation. If you want to innovate, you must create. Innovation is creativity applied. It's the way you take your good ideas and make money. Nourish your pocketbook, and you nourish your soul—all at the same time.

WHAT ARE YOU MISSING?

Often one of the reasons you don't innovate is you don't see that it's a priority in your life. Work Less, Make More comes down to seeing the possibilities. Identifying the options that are available and creating something new or different. That's what I call innovating.

I've outlined four powerful questions that will help you identify what opportunities you're missing by staying with the status quo. This part of the book is focused on making more. Can you really make more if you're not doing something different?

Ask yourself these questions.

1. What will happen to you if you fail to innovate? Be specific.
2. How are you already more innovative than your competitors? *If you work for someone else, your competitor is anyone who could take the next promotion you want.*
3. What do they do that is more innovative than what you do?
4. What was the latest new idea you developed that you considered innovative?
5. Did you actually implement that idea?
6. If the answer is no, what stopped you? And was that a good reason?
7. How much money do you think you're losing by not taking advantage of a new and better way of operating your business? *Do you even have a way to figure this out? If the answer is no, now's the time to find out.*

8. How much more money could you make if you developed a new idea that just 50 percent of your customers bought? *Don't get caught up in the details. Think big and dream a little. What's possible?*

It's very powerful to stop and think of the payoff you would be getting if you did focus your attention on innovation. If you think back to Chapter 3, Harness the Power of Focus, innovation is the activity you engage in when you're focusing on current or future customers. Innovation can be a priority with the system you've already developed.

HOW TO INNOVATE

How do you learn to innovate? I do not believe you wake up one morning and say, "Today I'm going to be innovative." That's not how it works.

Innovation comes from necessity. You create ideas to fill a need. That need is something someone else wants and is willing to pay for. When you're focused on innovations, you're focusing on making more. The single best way to make more is to come up with something new. A new product. A new service. A new twist on something. A new marketing approach. Something different from or better than what's already available.

The responsibility to innovate is up to you. You can't wait for someone to give you an innovative idea. If you keep waiting, it may never show up. Innovation is about taking responsibility to develop a new idea to fit a need. Being able to do that belongs to you.

Here are the things you need to keep in mind when you're training yourself to become an innovator.

Believe in Yourself

Many of you wish you could be more creative. You need creativity to come up with innovations, that's for sure. Many times you sense you *are* more creative, but you're unable to tap those creative juices. *I'm here to tell you that you are creative.* Creativity is not reserved just for writers, artists, and musicians. The difference between creative people and those who are not is simply a problem with beliefs. If you believe you're creative, you are. If you don't think you're creative, you're not. The same goes for innovation. If you think you can be innovative, you will be. If you think you can't be, you won't.

Think back to a time when you were a kid, filled with creativity and curiosity. Researcher G. M. Prince found that 90 percent of all five-year-olds tested as highly creative. The number dropped to 10 percent by the age of seven, and past age eight, the number dropped to just 2 percent. By the time you're 30, do you rank yourself as highly creative? What about when you're 40 or 50 or 60?

What happened to you? You were told to color within the lines. That's what grown-ups do when they color, so if you wanted to grow up, you did what you were told. As your education increased, your creativity probably decreased. You started to believe that your intelligence should be able to solve all your problems. You started using your logic like problem solving, dissecting, and analyzing. There was no room for creativity in business, you learned. Soon you began wearing the right suit, taking the safe road, and spouting the company line.

After all those years, if you aren't acknowledged for being creative, your creativity runs and hides. I know; it happened to me. For years, I was told the way to success was to follow the path that everyone else took. You know the one. Go to college. Major in something "sensible." Get a job in corporate America. Climb the corporate ladder. Someday you'll retire—and then you can draw and write and create.

I distinctly remember an experience when I was working in corporate America. I had just come back from yet another useless performance evaluation, and I was upset. My manager had told me I needed to stop thinking outside the box so much and follow the company culture more closely. He was basically telling me to be less creative. With managers like that, it's no wonder we don't believe we're creative. (You can clearly see why I had to leave and go work for myself. But please understand, you don't have to leave your job to be more innovative. We work with hundreds of clients of Work Less, Make More in their current jobs. I use this story just as the reason why I thought I wasn't creative. For many years, I didn't.)

The key to innovation is to stoke your creative fire. The flame may have died down a lot during the past few years, but it's still there—ready to burn again. It all starts with belief. Believing that you have what it takes to develop the next million-dollar idea. Or at least a great solution to a tough problem.

Have Passion for What You Do

What on earth does passion have to do with innovation? It has everything to do with innovation. *Everything.*

In my very last corporate job, I worked for a large cellular company. My job allowed me to add my own slice of innovation to whatever I was doing. I had the authority, the budget, and the space to create some great things. But did I? No. The reason was I really didn't care if the company was successful or not.

I remember sitting in a meeting where we were talking about customer retention and how many customers had left the month before. All I could think about during this long, drawn-out meeting was: "So what?" I was bored out of my mind, listening to a conversation I had little interest in. I looked around the room trying to see into the eyes of the people sitting near me. Did they have any passion for the conversation either? Was I the only one who thought I was going to scream? Turns out the answer was yes. I noticed they did care about these issues, so the problem had to be me.

In that state of mind, could I come up with solutions to decrease customer turnover? Of course not. I didn't have passion for that work, which is one of many reasons I don't work there anymore. In fact, I was so bored in that job, I just couldn't get my creative juices to flow.

Compare that experience to the company I own now. I'm in

the forefront of innovation in my industry, because I'm passionate about coaching. Passionate about success. Passionate about helping people live to their full potential rather than wallowing in mediocrity. I can easily create and innovate because I have passion for what I'm doing. It happens naturally and effortlessly, and it all stems from passion.

Do you have passion for your work? If you don't, go out and find something you can be passionate about. You simply won't innovate—or be fulfilled—unless you do. Go back to Chapter 2, Do What You Do Best, if you need some help in this area.

Expose Yourself to the New and Different—Every Day

An incredibly important part of being an innovator is having access to new and different stuff every day. In Part I of this book, Work Less, you focused on clearing out space in your life to focus on what's most important. When you're focusing on being more innovative, what's important is surrounding yourself with new experiences. If you don't stoke your creative fire, you'll lose that spark. The best way to light your fire is to expose yourself to something new all the time.

Turn the page for some examples.

What are you waiting for? Go out and give yourself a new experience.

Be a Lifelong Learner

That means get rid of the words *I already know that.* True innovators understand that they don't know anything. Creative ideas often come when we look at the same old thing in a new way. You just can't do that if you're shut off. Arrogant. Walking around saying, "I already know that."

If you're not open to learning new stuff—even learning the subtleties about what you already know—you won't innovate. It's not possible. Innovation is about being open to new ideas. Sometimes those new ideas are actually old ideas in disguise.

I used to have a client who was an engineering consultant.

Do Something Different Today

- Take a different route to work.

- Spend an hour playing with a six-year-old. Eat grass. Climb trees. Color with crayons on the wall. Do anything and everything the kid does.

- Spend $20 on magazines you've never read and about subjects you have no interest in. Read them and find three ideas you can apply to your own business or life.

- Run to the nearest bookstore and read a pile of Dr. Seuss books.

- Distribute whoopee cushions at the office and use them.

- Spend an hour surfing the Internet.

- Invite someone you barely know to visit a new restaurant with you.

- Go to work two hours early. Why? You just never know what will happen when you show up at the office at 6 A.M.

- Start every meeting with a joke. Have fun looking for the perfect joke.

George could have been a great consultant. He had a lot of knowledge about a lot of technical things, and companies paid him a high price to share his services with them. The problem was George had an "I already know that" attitude. He was the type of fella I would call uncoachable. (That explains why he didn't last long as a client.) No matter what book he picked up or who he spoke to, he simply shut himself off from learning anything new. He would often roll his eyes and say, "Oh, I already know that."

Do you think his success lasted? Of course not. The world

changed fast around him, and his competitors beat him at his own game: information. They stayed ahead of the trends and were able to give their clients exactly what they needed to stay competitive. George was left behind because he thought he already knew everything he needed to know. The last I heard, he was working tremendous hours trying to get some of his lost business back. That's not the secret to working less and making more.

If you think you already know it, you'll miss the opportunity. You see, innovative ideas are subtle. When I hear someone say, "I already know that," I immediately know they do not have what it takes to be a success. There's a sense of arrogance about them, and they're closed off from learning. Most of the time, the people who say, "I already know that" are the ones who may know it, but they do not *live it*.

Being a lifelong learner is not about carrying useless trivia around in your head. It's about living what you already know. You may think you know something, but you don't apply it, and you don't integrate it into your life. So you really don't understand it at all. To understand, you must experience. You must live. When you say, "I already know that," what you're *really* saying is you don't get it at all.

The game of working less and making more is not just about saying the right things; it's about doing the right things. That's right, applying and integrating *what you already know*.

How exactly do you do that? By learning from everything that happens to you. Here are a few guideposts to help you become a learner.

- Do you surf the 'net regularly?
- Do you read the new books out on the market?
- Do you ask yourself, "What can I learn from this?" when something goes terribly wrong?
- Do you subscribe either via e-mail or snail mail to at least five periodicals?
- Do you ask yourself, "What can I learn from this?" when something is a big success?

- Do you write in your journal every day reflecting on what you learned that day?
- Do you make sure that when you're giving advice, you're living the advice you're giving?
- Do you pay attention to the wake-up calls in your life and take action to prevent a crisis?

Do you have some work to do? Write down the 10 things you can do to become a lifelong learner in your journal. Study them monthly. Don't just read this book. Go out and take action. Apply what you're learning. Integrate it into your life. That will go a long way to helping you become more innovative.

Create an Inspiring Environment

Look around your office. Have you created an environment that reflects your personality? Really spend some time looking around your office and your company. Would a free-spirited, innovative hotshot want to work here? If not, why would you?

Place is essential to creativity. Not so small that it can limit you, but not too big that you get lost without the intimacy. If you're looking for that creative spark, change your environment so you change.

One of my clients began to understand how powerful her environment was to her as soon as she started a home-based business. Like many other people, Kathy created an office in her home. She carefully selected a desk, bookcase, computer table, and filing cabinet to house her things. Kathy chose a conservative paint for the walls, and basically duplicated the office she used to work in when she was an employee for someone else. Her home office looked like an office.

Because she was starting a new business, Kathy spent a lot of time in her office. She soon discovered that she was falling into the trap of working all the time without having much fun in her new business. Kathy had left her job so she could get some more joy in her life, and here she was, burned out all over again.

Her business required her to develop new products for her clients, but her ideas began to be flat. She didn't understand why.

When I asked her about her environment, Kathy told me it looked like a typical office. I said, "That's the problem. What can you do to liven up the place?" The light bulb came on. The next week Kathy told me she had completely overhauled her office. She had moved in comfortable furniture, painted the walls a bright color, lit fragrant candles, and played great music when she wasn't on the phone. The minute Kathy walked into her office, her creative juices started flowing again. It was as simple as changing her environment.

What can you do to alter your environment? Here are a few things to think about when you're building the ideal place for you and your creativity.

Color

Does the color make you sparkle with new ideas? Color has an amazing effect on people. Notice what happens when you walk into an office that's bright white. Do you feel tense and uneasy? A more important question: Would that color enable you to tune into your creativity? Use colors that reflect who you are.

Light

Think about changing your light to fit your different moods. Don't just use the stuffy old fluorescent light. What about sunlight? Soft lighting? Bright light? Use different lighting schemes at different times for best results.

One of my clients really has issues with light. Jim has an office in the basement of his home, and the light down there is horrendous. He noticed whenever he was in his office, he would get easily upset and frazzled. Yet when he moved upstairs to the dining room, which had two huge picture windows, his mood immediately changed. Jim invested in powerful lighting that mirrored natural light, and it made all the difference.

Toys

What can you play with to help you open up your mind? My husband Steve is quite a collector of toys. He has plastic iguanas in his office, plastic frogs sitting on the dashboard of his car, dinosaurs scattered throughout our kitchen, and a whole slew of his favorite books on hand. One day he asked me to make a flowerpot for the plant in his office (which, incidentally, he named Rudolph), and his only requirement was that I glue plastic bugs all over the pot. I did.

Music

Music can have a powerful impact on your creativity. Does a relaxed sound allow you to open your mind, or do you prefer something upbeat and lively? Many of my clients find it hard to relax, so they invest in subliminal music (you can find cassettes or CDs in the large bookstore chains) that occupies one part of the brain while the others are focused on creativity.

Invest in a portable CD player and use it whenever and wherever you go to create.

Smell

One of my clients swears that using different aromatherapy candles in her office really helps her come up with new and different ideas. I personally like the smell of cinnamon. It makes me feel as if I'm in a warm and comforting place.

Stuff That Hangs on Your Wall

If you came into my office, you'd find lots and lots of stuff plastered all over my walls. Inspiring quotes. Funny pictures. Love notes from my husband. By taking two seconds to look up, I'm automatically in a more creative mood.

What can you hang up today that will make you feel that way, too?

Comfortable Furniture

If you can't kick back and just think, you've got the wrong furniture. Go out and buy something comfortable to sit on. Or sit on the floor on big pillows. Get comfortable.

Clothes

The same goes for clothes. I just can't innovate if I'm all dressed up. Forget about the formal dress policy at work. Wear jeans and a T-shirt. Your flannel pajamas. Train yourself to be more innovative by feeling more innovative in your clothes.

Spend some time visualizing what your ideal office space looks like. There's no reason why you can't add a touch of who you are to your environment. Pull out your journal and detail what will make you feel more innovative.

Create Some Space in Your Life

The innovative ideas you're looking for often come when you slow down rather than speed up. Yes, you're trying to make more right now, you don't want to wait for the next idea, yet many times your best ideas come when you're not trying so hard.

Space plays a key role in the innovation process. If you have a glass full of water, you can't add any more. But if you pour some of the water out, you have space for more. Your mind is exactly the same. Making space allows your creative mind to fill the gap.

You've all done it before. When you stopped crawling and starting walking, you gave yourself space to learn something new. You didn't just crawl so fast that you started walking. No. You gave yourself some real room to unlearn crawling and learn how to walk. You *had* to quit crawling. And then you had to quit walking so you could learn how to ride a bike. You gave yourself the space to try something new.

Innovating is no different. Quit using your old behaviors so you can learn the new ones. Experiment. Be willing to fail. Give yourself the space to try something new. One of the best ways to create space in your life is schedule in time to do nothing. Just 15 minutes a day to sit and think. You'll stop your old behavior of rushing around trying to find the right answer, and instead you'll learn how to create some space for something new.

WHAT YOU NEED TO INNOVATE

If you remember back to the first page of this chapter, I wrote that innovation cannot happen without a need. You don't just walk in one day and innovate. There has to be a reason to create the new idea.

The most effective innovators use their customers' problems as the focus of their innovative ideas. Value, from the preceding chapter, spoke about that. Developing solutions to your customers' problems is a huge part of making more. And developing those solutions through products, goods, and services is how we innovate.

To make the most of any innovative idea, there are a few rules of thumb you'll need to follow.

A Supply of Good Ideas

Innovation requires a massive supply of good ideas. Yes, a massive supply. One idea leads to another idea, which leads to another. The more ideas you—and your team—can generate, the greater your chance of success. There are lots of great books out in the marketplace on how to generate ideas, so I won't go into them now.

A Team Approach to Innovation

The key to any innovative organization is the power of the team. Sure, you can innovate on your own, but the real power comes from a tremendous supply of good ideas. A massive amount of ideas usually comes from teams of people.

When you're organizing your creative team, design it like a basketball team, not a football team. Traditionally, American businesses operated like a football team. In football, you'll find narrow specialization: linebackers, centers, tackles, running backs, even special teams. Yet basketball puts special emphasis on generalized skills. As my assistant, Pat, says, everyone on the court has to dribble, pass, rebound, and shoot.

In football, the team regroups after every play to listen to one player (usually the quarterback) and the coach dictate what's going to happen next. In basketball, the game is too dynamic to regroup after every shot. Basketball players keep playing and improving as they go along. The basketball team approach is much more effective in developing innovative ideas. You need the team members to have general skills, learn as they go, and improve the more they practice. Don't set yourself up to be the only one telling the team what to do. You're stifling creative ideas that could lead to innovative products and services.

What if you don't have a bunch of employees to work with? Go out and find the best of the best and create your own nonemployee team. What about the vendors you work with? What about the strategic partnerships you're creating with other companies? What about developing your own mastermind of like-minded professionals who meet once a month to come up with innovative ideas? Don't let the fact that you work by yourself stop you from developing a strong team.

I tell my business owner clients to set up their own advisory boards, which is an automatic innovation team. Think of this advisory board as your own personal inner circle filled with people you respect and admire. Take the time to select those people you want to be part of this elite group. Can you really be honest with them about your situation? Have you collected some of the most creative people you know? Seek out people who are more innovative than you are and ask for their help.

You can also do this if you work within an organization. The key is for you to start the innovation group and take responsibility for its success. Don't tell me you can't do it. Of course you can. You just need to be creative in your approach.

An important part of selecting your innovation group is making sure they understand your expectations. When they make the commitment to be a part of your support team, they're agreeing to provide honest feedback, meet on a regular basis, and communicate in a timely manner with you. Be sure they're committing to *really* being a part of your team. It's then up to you to give them all the information they need about your business and to plan the brainstorming sessions. Take the responsibility and create your own team of innovators.

Stay Close to Your Customer

I've said it before and I'll say it again: You innovate for a reason. The best way to find the reason for your innovations is to stay as close to the customer as possible. That means you learn so much about your customers that you can predict what they need before they even know it. Now that's innovative!

How do you do that? You ask them. You listen to their answers. You spend time working in their businesses experiencing what they experience. And you spend 80 percent of your time with your most important customers. It's common sense, but many times you get so caught up in developing creative ideas that you forget to come up with ideas your customers can use.

Innovation is about creating wealth, and your wealth comes from your customers.

Finally, the Great Motivator: Deadlines

Often the very best innovative ideas come to fruition because you simply need the answer. Your back is against the wall, and failure is not an option.

Did you see the film *Apollo 13?* Everything possible went wrong on that flight to the moon, including a problem with a filter that reduced carbon dioxide levels. The only way to keep the three astronauts alive was to come up with a way to fit a square filter into a round hole. It seemed an impossible task. Yet the engineers had to find an innovative solution, or three men would die. Their backs were against the wall, and they found the solution. They innovated because they *had* to.

War is often a great motivator for innovations. The Germans in World War I developed a new marine propulsion system that replaced paddle wheels. The idea had been around for 100 years, but no one had a powerful enough reason to perfect the technology. Until the war, that is. In this case, they either innovated or they died. Literally.

Many people innovate because they force themselves to meet their own self-imposed deadlines. The best way to meet a deadline is to go out and tell a whole slew of people what you're going to do. Force yourself to hit a deadline. You'll be amazed with the innovative ideas that show up.

The great part of getting to this point in the Work Less, Make More journey is that innovation is a vital key to your future success. Masters wait for the day when they can innovate in their industries and professions.

So far in this book, you've taken the time to focus your life on what's most important, and it's freed up time to allow you to be more creative. Applying that creativity to being more innovative gives you the opportunity to make more money. Seeing and acting on new possibilities are part of getting to the place where you Work Less, Make More. It's up to you to use your creative powers to keep yourself there. In a word, innovate.

Exercises

1. Take out your journal and examine your beliefs about your own creativity. Have you been a champion for your own creativity or have you been a crusher? Who first believed that you were creative? Who told you that you weren't? How do these beliefs stop you from working less and making more?

2. Make a list of 100 things you can do to give yourself a new experience. How can you expose yourself to new stuff to constantly feed your creative mind?

3. Go out to a toy store this afternoon. Wander through the aisles and buy toys that resonate with you. Maybe you want to get a big box of crayons or some plastic bugs or silly putty or an action figure. Take it into your office and put it in a place of honor.

4. Open up your journal and capture in writing what your ideal office setting looks like. Vividly describe the environment that will allow you to be the most creative. Take one piece of that vision and incorporate it into your office.

5. Who do you need on your innovation team? Pick up the phone and invite at least five people to join you for an afternoon of brainstorming. Be selfish. Ask them to brainstorm your projects and ideas. Let them know you would be happy to return the favor.

6. Pick up the phone or stop by to see your top five customers. Ask them what products and services they want that you haven't yet provided. If that doesn't lead to any innovative ideas, ask them to describe their biggest frustrations with you. Take that problem to your innovation team and brainstorm how you can solve your customers' problems. Their problems could be the catalyst for a new innovation.

7. Take 30 minutes today to sit and be quiet.

CHAPTER 9

Generate High Income Now

Okay, admit it. Rather than take the time to progress through the book, some of you immediately jumped to this section. "I want high income right now," you said. "If only I made more money, everything would work out."

Do not be fooled. Your problems will not be fixed if you only made more money. If you haven't carved out time and space to come up with creative ideas to make more money, you won't do it. If you haven't figured out what you do best and maximized that, you won't do it. If you don't have the right people and the right technology in place, you won't do it. If you . . . Get the idea?

In fact, I often see people who go chasing after money, and it always eludes them. Or worse, they chase the money, get it, and the rest of their lives fall apart. One of my clients learned this lesson the hard way. When Don had graduated from college, he decided to go to work at his father's real estate company. Don had just gotten married and was expecting a child within the year; he wanted to provide for his family. He was pretty good at talking with people, and he decided he could make a lot of money in real estate. If you ask Don why he went into real estate, he won't tell you he loves people or that he gets charged up talking about properties. He'll tell you he makes great money. And his goal from the beginning was to make tons of money.

For any of you who are in real estate, you understand how many hours are involved in building your business. When everyone else is working, you're not. When everyone else is not working, like on nights and weekends, you are. Don soon found his business booming, and the time with his family dwindling. He was able to carve out some time to spend with his daughter, but his wife was another story. She worked the typical workday, so Don was lucky to spend a few hours with her each week. When she complained about their lack of time together, Don would get frustrated. He often said, "Just hold on for a little bit longer. I'm right on the verge of making it financially, and when I do, we'll be able to spend lots of time together."

During those years, Don believed his father when he said, "You have to sacrifice for your success." Don believed the motivational speakers who told him to never give up on his dream of being rich. Don believed the stories he heard about people overcoming tremendous odds to reach their goals. And Don did exactly what they told him to do. He sacrificed time with his family for his goal.

His wife stayed with him for ten years. In that time, Don took over his father's business and grew his own income to more than $300,000 a year. He worked on average 70 hours a week, and it was rare that he was home for dinner with his family. In fact, he told me that in that ten-year stretch, he only attended five events at his children's schools. That's one every two years. Yet the entire time he kept telling himself he needed persistence to stay focused on his goal.

The day Don hired an office manager to take over the day-to-day operation of the business, the day he decided he had finally reached his goal, he rushed home to share the news with his wife. Finally, he was in a position to be able to spend more time with her because his goal of being financially independent had come true.

That was the day she told him she wanted a divorce.

Going for a high income is not always the right answer. If you haven't read the first eight phases of the Work Less, Make More process, go back and start doing the work that's necessary. Creating high income is only part of the process. It's not the ultimate destination. You must do the other work I've outlined in this book in order to build the foundation to make more money. If you don't, the money machine you build will come crashing down.

What I want for you is to have high income without sacrificing who you are, without sacrificing the relationships in your life. Much of the work you've done getting to this place in the book will allow you to do just that.

I'm assuming if you're still reading, you've done the work you need to do in order to start making more money. The three chapters before this one (on duplication, value, and innovation) will help you to immediately generate more income. This section is about ensuring that you generate the highest income possible while investing the least amount of time. You must add value. You must innovate. And you must learn how to duplicate yourself. This section ties all the pieces together.

GIVE THE MOST VALUE AND ASK FOR THE HIGHEST PRICE

If you want to make more money, it's time to ask for more money. Yes, the easiest way to generate high income is to make more money. That means that right now I want you to ask for more than what you're currently making. Today. This week. Right now.

Don't start giving me excuses. Most people I work with can dramatically increase their incomes by asking for a raise from their employers or raising their prices.

I have never seen a company go out of business because its prices were too high, but I sure have seen companies go out of business because their prices were too low. The same thing is true for being employed. If you aren't being paid more than what you're worth by your current employer, there's a good chance you won't be there for long.

When you're focused on being the best, part of that means you charge the most for your services. You can afford to charge a higher price because you are simply that good, and people will pay for your services.

The great thing about asking for a raise or raising your fees/prices is it forces you to be worth that much. Do you get that? It forces you to be worth that much. You see, we all have it in our heads what people who earn $100,000 or $250,000 or $500,000 or $1 million a year are like. How they think, how they act, who they are. When you force yourself to play that game of being worth more, you suddenly become more. You change how you act, what you think, and who you are. Raising your price in the marketplace is the single best way to make sure you upgrade who you are to be worth that much.

One of my clients who happens to be a coach was having a problem attracting new clients into her practice. Sally was maintaining an average-size client base, and she went through a time when everyone she spoke to told her they couldn't afford her services. Sally was frustrated, and she began to question her abilities.

"Maybe I'm charging too much," Sally said. "It just doesn't make sense. I know I'm very good at what I do, and I just don't understand why they can't see it." If you were in the same situation, what would you do? Most people would react to this string of events and offer the same service for less money.

Wrong. What I requested Sally to do was raise her prices. I knew she was giving tremendous value for what she offered, and raising her prices would attract the right clients into her life who could afford her. Too many people were wasting her time talking with her about coaching when they simply could not afford it. Guess what happened? Sally added ten new clients during a six-week period.

When she had raised her prices, Sally immediately felt as if they were finally at a level that she deserved. At her old pricing, she often felt as if she offered way more than what she was getting paid for. When she would explain how much she charged, she felt almost embarrassed at the old pricing because she knew she was worth more. Sally was just afraid to ask for more. This simple shift allowed her to confidently ask for the business, and she got it.

Now there's an important point I need to make before I move

on. Yes, making more money is as easy as asking for it. But you must make sure you don't just ask for more money without thinking about the value you're providing.

Remember, you get paid for results. You don't get paid for how much time it takes. Let me give you a classic example. I have a client named Dirk who is the vice president of sales for a billion-dollar company. We were discussing his upcoming performance evaluation to help him organize his thoughts in order to get the most from the time he was spending with his boss. The first question I asked him was, "What results have you delivered in the past year?"

He said, "Results? It's my annual review. I know I'll be getting a raise. I just need you to help me justify what I want." As if he deserved it because he'd been there for 12 months. Yes, Dirk was in an interesting position. He had spent the last year reorganizing the sales team to get better results. Long term, he would get great results from his efforts. But that wasn't going to help him in the performance evaluation. It was difficult for him to identify specific results he had produced in a year of reorganizing, reformatting, and restrategizing.

If you find yourself in a situation like Dirk's, be sure to negotiate on the front end measurable benchmarks during a year of reorganization. You get paid for results, not just for being there. And when push came to shove, Dirk knew he hadn't delivered the results the company pays him for. Will he deliver in the future? Absolutely. But he doesn't get paid for putting in his time.

Remember: Dirk is a well-read, very intelligent, highly successful VP of Sales. If he can fall into the trap of believing time equals success, you can, too.

Become the best and raise your price in the marketplace. That's always been the secret to making more.

HAVING MORE THAN ENOUGH

I'd like to introduce you to a concept that means everything when it comes to having a high income. It's called reserve. Having a *reserve* means having more than enough. Yes, more than enough.

It's about having so much that you don't need any more. In fact, you have so much you easily and gratefully give it away, and there's still an abundance left over.

Having a reserve applies to having more than enough money. It also applies to having more than enough love, opportunities, friendships, happiness, business, time, and energy. Earlier in this book, I use the term *wealth* to encompass all the areas in your life. Think of reserve as an abundance of wealth. I'll be focusing the majority of my attention on having a reserve of money, but I've included two exercises in the back of the chapter to help you build a reserve in other areas of your life.

Why is having a reserve of money so important? Let me explain it this way. When you have money pressures, what usually happens is you start thinking about money *all the time*. You're constantly thinking you don't have enough money. You may even become consumed by the fact that you don't have enough money. You cannot make the right choices with your life because you're living with the fact that you don't have the money. You're focused on just surviving. You say no to opportunities with friends because you don't have the money. You say no to buying what you want because you don't have the money. You say no to giving anything to anyone else because you don't have the money. Not having enough money is a horrible experience to have.

Not having a reserve of money forces you to focus on survival. Working less and making more is not about surviving; it's about living. If you don't have a reserve of money, you can't live the life you want to live.

I know very well what not having enough feels like. My first business venture turned out to be the greatest experience of my life—and it also cost me a personal loss of $65,000 when I was just 26 years old. Yes, my business failed. It failed big time. It was the best experience because I learned what not to do in a business, and the lesson was an expensive one.

When my husband and I realized we were $65,000 in debt, we had two choices. One was to file bankruptcy, and the other was to pay it off. We chose the latter. For two years, we ate macaroni and cheese in a box because it cost only 59 cents. We stopped having friends because we thought we couldn't afford them. How embarrassing to tell someone you can't afford to go out to the bar for a cocktail! We stopped traveling. We worked our butts off to pay down the debt. But, just as importantly, we learned that to be successful, you must love what you do. I didn't love my first business. I just loved the idea of having my own business. There's a big difference.

Not having enough is not the place I want any of you to be. The day the debt was gone is a day I'll never forget. I felt as if I had my life back, as if the chains that were choking me were finally broken. Did I have to feel as if I were being strangled just because I was in debt? No. Not having enough felt that way to me, and I chose to handle the situation in that way. I could have responded to the debt load in a much healthier way, but I just didn't know then what I know now.

The single best way to create high income is to understand that money means freedom, especially when you're focused on working less and making more. The choices you'll make when you're going for freedom are much different from the choices you'll make if you're going for image. Having a reserve is about creating ultimate freedom. It's about freeing yourself from ever worrying about money again.

When I talk about having a reserve of money, your definition and my definition may be different. More than enough for you is probably different from more than enough for me. At one time in my life, having more than enough meant not being in debt. I am not challenging you to give up the rest of your life for the pursuit of money. Of course not. I'm just making a point. Having a reserve of money allows you to live the life you want to live. Let's put you on the path of having more than enough. I know you want to be on the path of having more freedom in your life or you wouldn't be reading this book.

If you don't have the foundation in place to generate more than enough, you'll be like so many lottery winners. In five years most of them are broke because they didn't use their money wisely. Building a reserve takes time. It's part of the journey you're on when you're working less and making more.

What would it be like if you had more than enough money? I mean so much money that you wouldn't even think about money because you would know it's there. How much is enough? I'd like you to define when you know you have enough money.

Pull out your journal and ask yourself these questions.

1. What dollar figure do you need to have in mind, to have to feel as if you had enough? *For example, having one million dollars in liquid investments.*
2. How do you feel when you have enough money? *For example, I no longer feel my heart race when my credit card bill comes in.*
3. How do you know when you have enough? *I can take 12 months off and still have enough to live on for the next 10 years.*
4. What does a reserve of money mean to you? Be sure to put it in a way that you can measure. Be as specific as possible.

HOW TO BUILD RESERVE

Now that you've defined what having more than enough means to you, you can put together an action plan to start building that reserve. Some of you reading this book have already developed a plan for building financial independence. Yet there are few people I meet who set up their plan to have more than enough. We're talking about building a reserve here. This is a great time to go back to your plan and make adjustments. Building a reserve is serious business, and it's never a bad idea to make changes that get you there quicker and easier.

Perhaps your challenge is that you spend all the money you make—and then some. The credit card debt is piling up, and you're feeling the pressure. That's obviously the exact opposite of what you're going for in building a reserve. The good news is that you can start building a reserve right away. There's no need to wait until your debt is paid off. Building a reserve is about paying yourself first. Trust me. You can start today.

If you need specific direction in helping you overcome your stumbling blocks with money, go to the Resources section in the back of the book. I've included some great books you need to start reading. I strongly recommend that you hire a professional to help you get your financial house in order.

What's needed to build that reserve of money? Your action plan may include the following:

- Reduce expenses. Why not reduce your expenses by 50 percent, take the extra money, and build the reserve?
- Change your investment strategy. Are you getting the return on your money that you should be earning?
- Take 10 percent from each paycheck and put it into a reserve account. Most people don't even notice the 10 percent once they get into the habit of putting it away.
- Create a new revenue stream where the monies are used only for your reserve account.
- Dramatically increase your profit margins on what you're already doing by cutting production costs, cutting selling costs, simplifying the process, or raising prices.

Pull out your journal and come up with 25 ways you can build a reserve starting today. What can you do today to get yourself on the right path?

There's a reason I didn't start off this chapter with how to increase your income. If you aren't building a reserve of money, it doesn't matter how much money you make—you'll always be broke. Start with the reserve first; then you can move to increasing your income to impact your lifestyle. This is not the time to say, "Someday when I make $X, then I'll start building a reserve." Many have tried later and failed. Don't let that be you.

GIVING IT AWAY ALLOWS IT TO COME EVEN FASTER

Go back to the list of ideas you have about building a reserve. Did you write that you were going to give money away? I can hear you gasp. Why would giving money away allow you to have more? Seems like an oxymoron, doesn't it?

Deepak Chopra, in his book *The Seven Spiritual Laws Of Success* (Amber-Allen Publishing, New World Library), describes money as energy. Money must be allowed to flow. He writes, "If we stop the circulation of money—if our only intention is to hold on to our money and hoard it—since it is life energy, we will stop its circulation back into our lives as well. Like a river, money must keep flowing, otherwise it begins to stagnate, to clog, to suffocate and strangle its very own life force. Circulation keeps it alive and vital."

You've probably heard this before: "The more you give, the more you will receive." It's true, not only concerning money but in the other parts of your life as well. Make sure your plan to build a reserve includes giving money away.

How much should you give away? That depends on you and your situation. At the bare minimum, give away 10 percent of your total income. Ten percent from all your sources of income. You can give to your favorite charity, your place of worship, your alma mater . . . it doesn't matter. My husband and I live by a philosophy that we give to anyone who asks. How can we turn down a six-year-old boy who comes to our home selling candy bars? We can't, so we give. Now that doesn't mean send your kid to knock on our door. Give where you feel it will matter.

When I share this concept with clients who are struggling financially, they often start to sweat. They immediately say, "Jen, I can barely pay my bills. How on earth can I afford to give 10 percent away?" All I can say is giving money away allows you to get more. Take Janice, for example. Janice was a single mom who was just barely covering her monthly costs. When we were working together, she had just changed careers to go into sales. Janice inherently knew that sales would give her the opportunity to make a nice living to support her family, and her brilliance was definitely the energy she gave off. People, especially her customers, simply loved to be around her.

One day I requested that Janice begin to immediately give 10 percent of her income away. I heard this gasp, and then she said, "Jen, do you really think that will make me do better in sales?"

My response was a resounding yes, so she took my advice. Janice wrote a check that day to the local animal shelter.

The next 30 days were a whirlwind for her. Every time Janice got a commission check, she took 10 percent out and gave it away. In that one month alone, she earned twice what she had earned the month before. Her income continued to rise for the next 12 months.

"Every time I wrote that check, I felt abundant. I somehow trusted the money would come back, and boy, did it," she says. "Giving money away was my secret to having an abundance in my life."

Giving 10 percent away allows you to accept more in your life. It allows you to upgrade who you are, and that's a powerful gift to give yourself.

USING THE POWER OF COMPOUND INTEREST

Money grows as a result of two forces: time and rate. Most people are so interested in increasing their income, they fail to focus on the most important thing, leveraging what they have already made.

Compounding is a vital concept if you want to maximize the money you're already making. Let me remind you of some examples of the power of compounding.

You're 30 years old, and you have $50,000 in investment monies. If you don't add any more to it, what will it be worth in 15 years—when you're 45 years old—at a modest 6 percent increase a year? The answer: $120,000.

What if everything remained the same and your earnings increased by 12 percent a year? The answer would double to $240,000, right? Wrong. Compounded interest would allow your money to grow to more than $273,000.

Let's pretend you now have $100,000 in investment monies. In 15 years, if you're earning 10 percent a year and you don't add any more to it, you'll have close to $418,000. In 30 years, at an average of a 12 percent return, you'll have close to $1,800,000. That's the power of compounding.

So what does this mean? It means a part of your financial strategy for having high income is to invest at least 10 percent of your income each and every month into an investment account that earns a minimum of a 10-percent return.

Do you need to know everything about the financial markets in order to invest your money? No, of course not. Go out today and find a financial consultant who can make your money work for you. I often see people who are afraid to even look at their financial strategy. If you want to work less and make more, a key component is learning how to harness the power of compounded interest.

Now pull out your journal and ask yourself this question if you're currently not investing 10 percent in yourself: "What holds me back from investing in myself each month? How does it serve me to stay this way?" If you are already investing 10 percent in yourself each month, ask yourself: "What can I do to increase my monthly contributions so I can build a reserve faster and more easily?"

Please go out and find professional help to teach you about compound interest. I only gave you a tiny bit to whet your appetite if you aren't investing money every month in your future. Take the time now to start a savings plan and work with a professional to get the best return on your hard-earned dollars.

BUILDING MULTIPLE SOURCES OF INCOME

When many of you took your first job, you made the mistake of putting all of your faith into one source of income. Many of you looked toward the day when you would retire after 35 years with the same company. "Then I'll be a millionaire," you told yourself. Maybe you weren't that naive, but many people still based their lives around one source of income. Their jobs or their businesses. They decided if they wanted a raise, they'd have to improve their performance. Get promoted or pick up new business. Raising their incomes was usually in their control, yet everything still rotated around that one source.

Now more than ever, having multiple sources of income is vital in today's world. During the past 10 years, millions of white-collar workers have been laid off. Their one source of income vanished in an instant. Some of you reading this book have experienced the trauma of losing your job. Those of you who work for yourself face the same thing. One day you're in business. The next day, maybe not. It's a reality.

Building multiple sources of income allows you to have more than enough. There's that reserve thing again. It gives you the freedom to have options if one of your income streams dries up. Having multiple sources of income is the single best way I know to build job security. Your security doesn't need to depend on one source. In fact, if you rely on one source of income, you're not building security at all.

For you entrepreneurs out there, take this idea and apply it to your businesses. Is one of your customers giving you more than 20 percent of your income? If so, you've set your company up to fail if that customer ever leaves. Start now to turn the numbers in your favor. The rule of thumb is not to allow one customer to constitute more than 10 percent of your total revenues. What shifts do you need to make to move your numbers to your favor?

The key to developing multiple sources of income is to make sure you don't spend more time than is necessary. Yes, you will need to invest your time to get something working. Yet if you start three profit centers that all require you to invest 30 hours a week, you've just signed up for a 90-hour-a-week job. That's not the secret to working less and making more!

Deciding what to build into a new income source is creative and fun work. Think of your new profit center as yet another way for you to use your brilliance. Imagine yourself in the middle of a wheel. At the center are all your strengths and abilities, the things you do extremely well. Each new profit center is a spoke coming off the wheel. It's connected to your strengths, but it adds a new dimension or a new twist to what you're already doing.

We're all familiar with a woman by the name of Oprah Winfrey. Here's a woman who hosts one of the most popular and influential talk shows in the country. Her brilliance is her ability to communicate with and for people. She's a *master* communicator. Yet Oprah does not make her living as just a talk show host. That would be relying on one source of income. She owns the production studio that produces *The Oprah Winfrey Show,* and the company syndicates the show to hundreds of TV stations across the world. She's used her communications skills to write two best-selling books, one with her personal chef and the other with her personal trainer. She's even taken her passion for physical mastery to the video stores by creating her own videotape.

It doesn't stop there. Her brilliance in communications has allowed her to buy the film rights to some of her favorite books, and she's in the process of producing the films or making them into made-for-TV films. Oprah even acts in them from time to time. There are probably other profit centers she's created that we don't even know about.

Why can't you create an empire like Oprah's? You can.

Ideas for Developing Multiple Sources of Income

Start building your own profit centers by integrating your brilliance along with innovation, adding value, and duplicating yourself. You will need to build a team to support your quest. You have tremendous knowledge to do all these things; now it's just a matter of putting them into action.

When you're thinking about developing multiple sources of income without adding in an incredible amount of time, here are a few ideas:

Royalties

Best-selling authors and famous musicians aren't the only ones who can generate royalties. You can invent a product and sell the rights to someone else to market and distribute. You can publish a book or audiotape series to sell and allow a distributor to sell your products.

The whole point is to base your earnings on future sales—that someone else does—and you go on to another idea.

Rental Income

Your biggest task once you have purchased the property is collecting the rent. Be sure to align yourself with a 24-hour maintenance company so you aren't bothered in the middle of the night with a tenant complaining of a broken toilet.

Selling Consumable Products

Consumable products are those that customers buy over and over again, like vitamins, cosmetics, and long distance and Internet services. Focus your attention on building up a customer base, and you'll find that you'll eventually switch your focus from selling to servicing your accounts.

Selling a Business You've Built

Too many entrepreneurs phase out their businesses or go out of business once they've lost interest in what they've created. Build a business that you can sell from day one.

Additional Products and Services for Your Current Customer Base

Your loyal customers know, like, and trust you, and there's a good chance they will buy additional products and services from you.

Residual Income

Ask yourself how you can set up your income stream to come from consistent or permanent sources. The cellular phone companies give away their phones so they get customers who will pay their monthly service bills forever. What can you do to build passive or consistent income?

How to Use Your Brilliance to Build Income

Let's start by brainstorming how you can use your brilliance to generate additional income. Get out your journal and start writing.

1. My brilliance is . . .
2. What are 25 new ways I can use my brilliance to generate

more money? *Go ahead. Use that creative, powerful mind of yours.*

3. Which of these ideas will cost the most money to get started? *That's probably not the one you want to start with.*

4. Which of these ideas will cost the most time to get started? *That's probably not the one you want to start with.*

5. Which of these ideas will cost the least money to get started? *This may be a good idea to start right away.*

6. Which of these ideas will cost the least time to get started? *This may be a good idea to start right away.*

7. What people do I need to talk with in order to get these ideas into action?

8. What can I do today to start building multiple sources of income?

Once you've flushed out your ideas, I recommend that you look at those that will bring you a 20 to 1 return. Rather than getting caught up in a new idea or strategy, first project how much revenue you will earn from the idea over a 10-year period. Use conservative numbers, and demand a 20 percent return on your time and money. This allows you to focus on those projects that will build your financial picture instead of getting caught up in a "good" idea that never pays off. Focus on high income when developing multiple sources of income. Make sure you're passionate about them, too. This journey is about working less, making more and *having fun.*

Exercises

1. Open your journal. Where in your life are you chasing money? What is it costing you to spend so much time and energy chasing it?

2. You've developed your definition of what a reserve of money means to you. What about a reserve of love, opportunity, space, and time? Write at least one page on what a reserve means to you in these four areas. What can you do today to build a stronger reserve in all areas of your life?

3. In this book, money means freedom. Do you believe that statement? Why or why not? Write for at least three pages about your beliefs.

4. Invest some time and research an organization that you would feel comfortable donating financial resources to. If you can, go visit that organization and see its operation. Get an idea of exactly where your money would go and who you would be helping. Then pull out your checkbook and give 10 percent of whatever you have. Even if it's $5, give the money away.

5. Brainstorm at least 100 possible sources of income. Go through and highlight the ideas that resonate with what you do extremely well. Which three ideas seem to be able to give you the greatest return on your time and energy?

6. Develop a plan to implement the three best ideas from the group. What resources will you need to implement these ideas easily and effortlessly?

7. What do you have to do with your current source of income to make space for another source? Take action and do it now.

CHAPTER 10

Develop Power Relationships

There's an old proverb that perfectly describes why relationships are so important in the Work Less, Make More journey.

If you want to be prosperous for a year, grow grain.
If you want to be prosperous for 10 years, grow trees.
If you want to be prosperous for a lifetime, grow people.

Work Less, Make More is about creating an easy, simple, and effortless lifestyle. It's about surrounding yourself with people who support who you are and who bring new opportunities into your life. It's about connecting at some level and knowing that your life is more because you met.

Developing strong relationships includes everyone you come into contact with: your customers, clients, vendors, suppliers, employees, friends, business associates, partners, coworkers, accountants, lawyers, bankers, mentors, neighbors, coaches, children, parents, spouses, *everyone*.

No matter how hard you try, you must work with other people in order to have success. You must work with others if you hope to work less and make more. You can't do it alone, so you have to learn how to connect with them.

You may be reading this chapter and saying, "Tell me something I don't know. Of course I need other people to be successful. I can't buy all my products and services myself." And you're right, you can't. But developing powerful relationships is not just about selling or working with other people. It's about connecting at a deep level that allows you to work less and make more. Relationships are the final key to this program.

One of my clients, Jeremy, took to this idea of harnessing the power of relationships. We had been working together a short time, and Jeremy was struggling with what to do with his business. He had made a name for himself in the financial management arena—he was a master at raising money for start-up companies—but he knew his real brilliance and passion could be found in the Internet. If only he could find the time to focus on it.

We were brainstorming one day on how he could build a transition plan between financial consulting and Internet marketing. Jeremy's first priority was to bring in strong cash flow to allow him to pay off a personal debt he had incurred before he could move into Internet work. Jeremy felt as if he would forever be pigeonholed into financial work, but I shared with him that if he built enough strong relationships with people who knew, liked, and trusted him, someone would give him the chance to do what he most wanted to do. He decided to take my advice.

During the next 90 days, Jeremy reached out and reconnected with folks he already knew. They introduced him to some new people, and he cultivated relationships with those he thought could help him. In that 90-day time period, Jeremy's income increased by more than 250 percent! All he had to do was use the power of relationships. Jeremy was well on his way to designing what he always wanted to do.

Was it really that easy for Jeremy to reach out and find the right people? Well, yes and no. Jeremy's big stumbling block in trying to go into the Internet field was he didn't feel as if he knew that much about it. He was afraid to talk to people about his ideas because he didn't feel he could impress anyone enough to believe in him. And he was right. What Jeremy did instead was connect with who these folks were as people, and he built his relationships on that human bond.

For most of you, there's one big thing that gets in your way of connecting, really connecting, with other people. It's the thing that prevents you from working less and making more, and it's harder than anything to admit it. It's the reason you think you want more money to buy the nice house. To drive the great sports car. To have the clothes that make you feel like a million bucks. To make you feel better about yourself.

Don't get me wrong. I want you to have these things. You deserve them. You should have them, but not if they're the only thing your life is about. Making more is about making more of your life. Part of that is connecting at a deep level with other human beings. The problem is, you prevent yourself from connecting because of one big thing.

The reason you don't connect is because you're too busy trying to impress. You're desperately trying to prove that who you are is good enough, so you fall into the trap of showing others how great you really are. It blocks the connection you could have, and it stops you from making more of your life.

THE IMPRESS ME GAME

It's very easy to identify the ways you try to impress other people. See the list on the following page.

The Impress Me Game can work. It often does. The problem with playing this game is you're competing with everyone else out there who's playing it, too. Someone else makes up the rules, and

How You Play the Impress Me Game

- Drive a fancy car.
- Tell how many clients/customers you have.
- Share how much money you made last year.
- Share how much your business has increased.
- Tell someone what you've accomplished.
- Wear expensive clothes.
- Rent a prestigious office—and make sure everyone knows it.
- Live in a high-rent district or pretentious neighborhood—and make sure everyone knows it.
- Pick up the tab every time you're out.
- Buy expensive, elaborate gifts.
- Tell about all the celebrities you know or have met.
- Flood someone with paper or e-mail to justify that you know what you're talking about.
- Casually drop that you graduated from Harvard or have an M.B.A. or law degree.

you run yourself ragged trying to impress more and more. It turns into a ruthless game of one-upmanship that sounds like:

"I have a Ph.D."

"I have two Ph.D.'s."

"I have two Ph.D.'s, an M.B.A., and have written a book."

"I have two Ph.D.'s, an M.B.A., have written 10 books, and my dad can beat up your dad."

What are the ways that you try to impress other people? Pull out your journal and write down the ways you get caught up in the Impress Me Game.

It's horrendous how much you diminish other people in some way just to justify to yourself that you're good enough. I see this happen over and over again with the very people hired to help you. For instance, personal assistants.

How many times have you bragged to your assistant about how much money you're making? How much free time you have off and how wonderful your family is? It's not what you say, but how you say it. It's as if you were saying your life is better than hers just because you're the boss.

Making other people feel inferior has nothing to do with connecting with them. It has to do with feeding your ego. You will not work less and make more until you put that ego away. The key to developing power relationships comes down to this: how you connect with other people. And how you connect is about showing that you're authentic. That you're human.

I've put together a few tips you need to know as you begin to develop stronger relationships. It's about learning how to connect with someone at a deep level. It's about creating such a powerful relationship that you learn just as much from them as they learn from you. It's about creating such a bond that the other person can't help but support who you are.

Here are some ideas on how you can shift from impressing to connecting.

Focus on Being Where You Are

Some people like to call this being in the present. What I mean by being where you are is when you're with another person, you're really with them. It drives me crazy when I'm at a cocktail party and the person I'm talking to is more interested in scoping out the room than he or she is in talking with me. They're focused on trying to impress everyone else because they're talking with me, and they want to make sure everyone notices them. Or worse, they're looking for the next person they want to impress. That's not the way to develop a powerful relationship.

With extremely busy people, not being in the present often

happens like this: When you're at home, all you're thinking about is how much work you have to do at the office, so you're not really with your family. And when you're at the office, all you can think about is being at home with your family. You can't develop powerful relationships if you aren't focused on what you're doing at the moment.

Take the time to tune in to the person you're talking with. I often take a deep breath and focus my attention on what he or she is saying. Yes, it's tough when you have hundreds of other things to do. At that moment, however, the most important person is the one you're with.

Commit to Not Knowing the Answer

This is really hard for some of you. One of the ways you try to impress other people is by sharing everything you know about a situation. You know, being the know-it-all. "I am the almighty, and I have all the answers." A big turnoff.

A great way to connect with someone is to admit that you don't know the answer. Instead, ask them what they think. I often do this when I'm coaching my clients. I may know the answer, but I'm more interested in helping my clients find their own answers. So I say, "I don't know. What do you think?" We connect because I'm genuinely interested in what they think, and my clients grow from the experience.

Be Authentic

Authenticity. I believe this is the most difficult one of all to master. You often try so hard to hide what doesn't work in your life that you mess up what does work. It's almost as if you were afraid you'll be found out. You're afraid that if someone finds out you're disorganized or have $10,000 in credit card debt, or got fired from a job, they won't like or respect you anymore. Worse, they won't see you as successful.

Connecting with someone is all about being true to who you are. It's about exposing that you, too, are human. I've personally worked hard on this. It took me almost two years to admit I lost more than $65,000 in the first business I started. Yet when I started to overcome my own shame of failing, other people saw me as a real success. Why? Because I survived and lived to tell about it. When I share my story, the other person usually shares a big failure he or she learned from, too. When I was so busy trying to impress people, I never would have thought that's how they'd react. Admitting that I failed opened up the doors to allow me to connect with other people.

Part of being human is admitting that you make mistakes. You aren't perfect. You think being vulnerable means being weak, so you pretend to be strong. What you forget is that no one will create a deep and rich relationship with you unless that person knows who you really are. People know when you are pretending, when you are covering up. Being authentic means honoring and showing who you truly are.

The key to remember is this: You are a living, breathing human first. A businessperson second.

Have you picked up on the underlying theme of learning how to let go of the Impress Me Game? The secret is learning to respect who you are just the way you are. It's about admitting that you aren't perfect, but you're at your best. It's about facing your fears and having the courage to admit you're afraid. It's about knowing in your heart that what you have to offer is powerful, and you're searching for people who understand that gift.

Working less and making more is about being honest with yourself and with other people. Through that honesty, you'll find opportunities arriving at your door based on the deep relationships you've created.

CREATING A POWERFUL RELATIONSHIP WITH FAILURE

When you think about relationships, you often think only about creating relationships with people. You also create relationships with many aspects of your life. What about building a powerful relationship with failure? That seems like an oxymoron, doesn't it? Building a relationship with failure?

Most people have a tremendous fear of failure. Instead, you hide from it. Deny it. Fear it. Ignore it. Avoid it. Hate it. Many people believe: If at first you don't succeed, destroy all the evidence that showed you tried.

All successful people know that a crucial key to success is learning how to fail. The freedom to fail gives you the opportunity to succeed. You probably won't be a success on your first try. If you accept that and instead look for the opportunity to learn, your failure becomes a huge success.

After my business failure, it took me a few years to realize that failure was *the single most influential moment* in my life so far. Those are big words, but it's the truth. By failing, I learned what not to do with a business. What industry I didn't want to invest in. Who I needed to trust and who I needed to stay away from. I learned more about cash flow, financial projections, good people, bankers, lawyers, salespeople, and myself than I ever could have learned from books or teachers. Experience became my most influential teacher.

When I look back on my life, I've learned more from failure than I ever have from success. Failure forces me to pay attention. To really figure out what is going on so I can make it work. Failure, if you develop a strong relationship with it, will allow you to pay attention and make the changes you need to make.

Many of you came to Work Less, Make More because something in your life wasn't working. You were failing, and you used that experience to find another way. Failure is a powerful part of your life. It always forces you to wake up.

Think back to a time in your life when you failed. Is it hard even to look at it? Ask yourself a few questions.

1. Describe an experience in which you failed. Vividly describe the details and the circumstances involved.
2. What did you learn from this failure?
3. How did learning that lesson enable you to move to a new and better place?

4. What did you learn about *who* you are?
5. What events immediately followed the failure, and what did you experience from them?
6. How did this failure allow you to succeed in the future?

Often, when I ask people to do this exercise, I get one of two reactions. They're excited to look at their failures in a new way, or they're scared to death because they've been deluding themselves. They pretend failures didn't even happen. No matter what your reaction is, learning how to develop a powerful relationship with failure teaches you to move forward and experiment. Taking risks is about being free. Learning how to love your failures allows you to be free.

Here are a few basic principles that can help you turn your failures into successes.

Look at Failure as a Step Toward Success

The problem with failing is that other people see your failures, too. Many companies post a huge, white board in their sales departments to show visually how each salesperson is doing each day. If you aren't having a good month, everyone knows it. Your failure is posted for all to see. The same thing goes for monthly reports that often circulate throughout corporate America. Your failures are there for everyone to evaluate, and often, we think people are judging us because we failed.

Most people are so worried about covering up their own failures they aren't worried about yours. Why do you think someone came up with the saying CYA (Cover Your Ass)?

It's embarrassing to fail. One of my clients has a tremendous issue with his failure. Brian spent many years working for a large Fortune 100 company, and about two years ago, he was promoted to national sales manager. It was the job he had been working toward for the past five years, and he felt as if he had finally arrived.

During his two years in that position, everything went wrong. His biggest client chose another vendor to work with. Employee turnover became a nightmare because the company was downsizing, and Brian wasn't given the resources he needed to fill vacant sales positions. When he went in for his performance evaluation, Brian was told he was doing a poor job. His vice president didn't acknowledge the external challenges the company created; he focused only on the fact Brian's team hadn't made quota.

Brian felt like a failure. When a buyout offer came across his desk, he took it and left the job he had worked so hard to get. It's been five years, and Brian still has a challenge talking about this experience. Let me clue you in on what's happened to him since he left that position. Brian took a job as a national sales manager for a software company and moved from Minnesota to California. He's making almost twice what he made at his old company, and his team performs on average at 110 percent of quota. Brian's failure forced him to look at some serious performance issues in his own life, and he hired me to help him become a more powerful leader. That's exactly who he's become. Yet if you ask him about the worst time in his life, he still focuses in on his failure at his old company.

I say that failure turned out to be the best experience in Brian's life because he learned who he was and who he wanted to be. It was the kick in the butt he needed to move toward the success he deserved. Only through that failure could he have found a company that would give him the resources he needed to succeed.

Before you start whining and pitying yourself for your failures, ask yourself an important question: "What have I learned from this?"

Failure Is Often a New Beginning

When I was a kid, my brother Dave and I used to play baseball or football with the neighborhood kids. We had this rule called *Do Over*. If something wasn't right—like the ball went out of bounds or someone was standing in the wrong place—rather than admitting failure, we just did a "do over." We played it out again. We loved Do Over because we could always find a reason to do it over if we failed somehow.

What if you did the same thing with failure? Just did it over? Failure is a great way to start anew. Many people like to analyze and overanalyze their failures. They look at every single thing they did wrong and use their failures as weapons against themselves. They use failure as a reason to stop. A reason to stay where they are. A reason to get stuck.

Failure gives you an opportunity to start again. To wipe the slate clean. Isn't that why they made erasers? To wipe the chalkboard clean. Rather than using failure as a weapon, use failure as a way to clear your head and start over.

Keeping failure in perspective allows you to appreciate that failure is the pathway to success. My personal philosophy has everything to do with failure. Fail sooner to succeed faster.

What's your philosophy about failure? Pull out your journal and develop your own philosophy about failure. The next time you feel as if you failed, pull out your philosophy and remind yourself why failing is just as important as succeeding is.

CREATING A POWERFUL RELATIONSHIP WITH YOURSELF

If you've been paying attention to the theme of this book, you've realized that the real key to Work Less, Make More comes down to one thing: developing a powerful relationship with yourself.

Remember the beginning of the book? I wrote: "The truth is you're very often working in order to avoid yourself, your feelings, your families, and your life." Having a powerful relationship with yourself allows you to tune in to yourself. To tune in to your feelings, your family and friends, your life.

If you don't know what you want, if you don't know where you're going, if you don't know what you think and feel, if you don't know what you want your life to stand for, if you don't know who is in your life to support you, if you don't know what will make you happy . . . how on earth do you expect to make it?

Developing a powerful relationship with yourself must be in place before you can create the lifestyle you want to live. I mean *really* want to live. Not the lifestyle you think you want until you get there and realize you paid too high a price.

We spent a lot of time in this book opening the door to help you create a relationship with yourself. The critical link to ensure you continue to work less and make more is building a strong relationship that will never crack. No matter how many things go wrong, a powerful relationship with yourself will always pull you through. It allows you to reach deep down inside and find the strength you need to redesign the life you want and deserve. It allows you to survive anything and everything life throws your way.

How do you take your relationship with yourself to the next level? That's a great question, and I have a few ideas.

Harness the Power of Silence

The single best way to deepen your relationship with yourself is to give yourself quiet time every day. How much quiet time do you really have? Most of you turn on the TV as soon as you get up in the morning to catch the news and weather. Your family, if you have one, is creating noise all around you. You then jump into your car and listen to the radio on the drive to work. At work, your phone rings off the hook. People are hustling and bustling all around you. You're surrounded by people all day. Then you go home. The TV is on, or your kids are running around, or you're off to a meeting or volunteer activity—again surrounded by people. If you exercise, you put on a headset and listen to music to occupy your mind. If you read, you're filling your head with other people's thoughts and ideas. You go to bed exhausted without taking time to listen to yourself.

Writing in your journal, a habit you've developed by this place in the book, is a great way to tune into yourself. It's time to bring the relationship with yourself to a new level. Harness the power of silence by giving yourself 20 minutes of it every day. Get up 20 minutes early, get a cup of decaffeinated coffee, and just sit and think. Learn how to meditate for 20 minutes a day.

What you put into your head first thing in the morning sets the tone for the day. Why do you listen to the radio or TV and all its bad news? Negativity first thing in the morning does have an effect on you. Set yourself up for success by listening to you. Shower and dress in silence.

Shut off the radio or CD player when you're in the car. Allow yourself to take time to tune in to your thoughts. Pay attention to how you talk to yourself. Are you critical? Supportive? Pessimistic? Friendly? Notice what you say to yourself. You'll discover that what's occupying your attention tells you a lot about what's truly important to you in your life. It could be a clue to some changes you need to make.

Let your mind take a break from the hustle and bustle at the office. Shut your office door. Turn off the phone and take 20 minutes just for you. If you can't get any quiet at the office, take a 20-minute walk. Alone. You'll come back refreshed and renewed.

Take 20 minutes before you go to bed, look out the window, and listen to what's going on inside. Acknowledge yourself for what you've done and who you've been today. Let your mind have a break and tune in to yourself. The peace and calm you'll experience will allow you to fill yourself up. Every day.

Base Your Life on Who You Are, Not What You Do

Have you ever met someone and the first thing out of his mouth is what he does? You know. "Hi. I'm Andy, and I'm a lawyer." Why do you have to tell everyone what you do for a living?

I don't mean to degrade or lessen the success you've had in your career. That success is a lot of the reason you're investing your time in Work Less, Make More. Building a powerful relationship with yourself has little to do with what you do. It has to do with who you are.

Many people—maybe you?—define themselves by the roles they play in life. They say: "I work for AT&T." "I'm the parent of two wonderful girls." "I'm married to a minister." Ask yourself this question: How much of your identity is tied up in what you do? If the answer is a lot, then you're letting your role define you. Your role is usually linked to your status and how people see you.

Andy's statement, "I'm a lawyer," lets him silently tell you he's educated, a professional, and a whole slew of other things you know about lawyers.

When you define your life by what you do, think of all the things that you aren't honoring. What about the fact that you're smart, witty, and have a passion for old books?

To create a powerful relationship with yourself, break yourself from defining who you are by what you do. You're holding yourself back from true success if you don't know who and what you're really all about.

I can feel your frustration coming on. You may be thinking that you've been doing a lot of work making time and space for what you truly want to do. Why do you have to do more work on yourself? Face it. Life is always about learning, changing, and growing. You didn't think I'd finish this book on an easy note, did you?

Creating a powerful relationship with yourself is what will help you maintain the changes you've made so far. More important, being in touch with who you are allows you to create a life that you want to live. It allows you to say no to the things that don't support you. It forces you to make choices for your own happiness and fulfillment. Developing a strong relationship with yourself is about freedom. Yes, freedom. Freedom to live the life you designed and created. Isn't that why you really opened this book in the first place?

How do you begin to identify who you are outside work? Pick up a pen and fill in this statement 20 times. Do not write what you do, just who you are. For example, *I am funny* is who you are. *I am a father* is what you do. Focus on the qualities of who you are.

1. I am _____

2. I am _____

3. I am _____

4. I am _____

5. I am _____

6. I am _____

7. I am _____

8. I am _____

9. I am _____

10. I am _____

What did you learn from this exercise? Open your journal and reflect on what you've learned.

Reflect on Where You've Been and Where You Are

This book is coming to an end, and I want you to get the most from your experience. Fight the urge to rush out and start doing something. Now's the time to savor your experience.

What I often see is people who are often so busy redesigning their lives to Work Less, Make More, they forget to take the time to savor the experience. They forget about what they've accomplished. Where they succeeded. Where they failed. Who they met. Who they became. They often spend more time looking at the future than they do the past. And they sometimes fail to learn the lessons they need to learn.

This material has a powerful impact on many people. If you've read this far and have done the work, you are not the person you were when you picked up this book.

Think about it this way: Your life is more than just setting and achieving goals. A lot more. Each part of you makes up the tapestry of your life. The pieces fit together to make a pattern. When you step back and look at your life, you'll notice that a pattern emerges. You may like the pattern. You may not. If one area negatively dominates your life, your overall life needs some work. The trick to making a breathtaking life is choosing the pieces that fit together.

Taking the time to *pay attention* to your life is the key, as you've seen me emphasize throughout this book. Noticing what's been happening helps you understand where you came from so you can prepare for where you want to go.

I challenge you to reflect on your experiences with Work Less, Make More. Pull out your journal and let's look at what's different.

229

DEVELOP POWER RELATIONSHIPS

Establish Where You Were

When you first picked up this book, what did your life look like? What were you concerned with? What were you thinking? Look at the 10 areas of your life: work, money, play, friends and community, family, intimate relationships, personal growth, spiritual and emotional, physical and health, and environment.

Notice How You Got Where You Are

Go back and reread your journal entries from the work you've done with this program. You'll begin to remember things you had forgotten. What's different about who you are now from when you started this book?

Reflect on What Work Less, Make More Means to You

After you've pieced your journey together, sit down with your journal. Reflect on what you think this material has meant to you. What is it you've let go of? How have you shifted your beliefs or your thinking? How has your behavior changed? What lessons have you learned? Who have you become?

Most important, what has changed since you started reading this book? Notice your changes in thinking, your changes in behaviors, your changes in how you see yourself, your work, and the world.

Notice Where You're Going

You've filled your head with a lot of information. How will your life be different now that you believe you can Work Less, Make More?

A word of caution: Don't get hung up on the part of your life you still don't like. Now's the time to appreciate and honor where you've been and where you're going. Where you're going is toward the life you've always wanted. The life I call Work Less, Make More.

Exercises

1. Start a new habit of waking up 20 minutes early every day. Grab your journal and write three pages. Write whatever comes to your mind. Allow your criticisms to show up on the page. Allow your positive thoughts to show up on the page. Make the commitment to yourself that you'll cultivate a powerful relationship with yourself every day.

2. How do you try to impress the people around you? Write about it in your journal. Why is it so important what others think about you? How do your fears get in your way of creating powerful relationships with other people?

3. Describe who you are at work and who you are at home. Are there any differences between who you are in both places? Take the time this week to let a little bit of your nonwork self show up at the office.

4. Describe a time in your life when you reacted poorly to a failure. Pull out your journal and rewrite the story. How could you have acted instead? Don't dwell. Just write.

5. Having the courage to risk is a part of being free, which means you must have a powerful relationship with courage. What is your philosophy of courage?

6. Ask yourself this question: "What is less looking like to me today?" Then ask yourself: "What is more looking like to me today?"

7. Go back and compare your answers with the ones you wrote when you first started this program. What has changed?

.

FINAL THOUGHTS

As our time closes, I'm struggling with how to end this book. I want to leave you with something that will encourage you to take action. To go out there and create the life of your dreams.

Sometimes it's hard to find the words for something I feel so strongly in my heart.

I wrote this book to give you the tools and strategies to find the freedom you are searching for. I wanted my words to compel you to find a different way, a better way, to live your life. I know you've worked hard on starting the process of redesigning your life, and by now you understand what those words Work Less, Make More truly mean.

Now it's up to you to make them *real*. These techniques, these strategies, these ideas are only as good as you make them, and it won't do you any good if you don't take action.

I know some of you out there will put down this book, and you won't apply one thing in your own life. You may even tell other people about this book, but you won't take action to change. This book will become just another thing you can cross off your reading list.

I don't want that to happen to you. The game of success is not just about reading the right things. It's not about saying the right things. It's about doing the right things. It's about applying and integrating *what you already know.*

If you take action, you can do anything you want to do. There is no limit to what you can accomplish. Please don't let anyone or anything make you believe otherwise. Work Less, Make More will be your reality. You need only to believe in yourself, then go out and make it happen.

I challenge you to make your life a masterpiece. Create an extraordinary life when every day you feel the freedom, the joy, the fulfillment, and the satisfaction you've been searching for. You'll never find what you're seeking if you're only focused on checking things off your To Do list or chasing more money. Life is about being who you really are. Having the courage to just be you when the world has gone crazy around you. That's what making your life a masterpiece is truly all about.

I hope we have the opportunity to meet someday, and you'll share with me the story of your life's success.

Make yourself proud. Make your life matter.

ACKNOWLEDGMENTS

No book is ever written alone, and I am forever grateful to the people who helped me write this material.

To Diane Menendez. You are a source of great wisdom and insight. To Madeleine Homan, my coach, who still believes in my big dreams when no one else does. To Rob Daumeyer, who gave me the opportunity to write a column that has opened up more doors than I can ever acknowledge. And to all the editors who use my material in your publications. Thank you.

To the Work Less, Make More pilot group: Angela Byington, Anne Lawley, Vickie Bevenour, J. D. Davids, Dror Moshkovski, Lori Stine, Melinda Short, Michael Catanzaro, Ruth Ann Bowers, and Susan Gulka. You were in the trenches with me when I was creating this book, and your feedback was invaluable. Thank you.

To the folks who offered to read my manuscript: You know who you are. You saw gaps and weaknesses I didn't see, and this book is a masterpiece because of your insights. To Pat Buede, a valuable friend and perfect assistant. To Jeffrey Gitomer, always brutal, always blunt, and always an inspiration.

To my publicist, Celia Rocks, and her amazing publicity team.

You are a true Work Less, Make More believer, and you help me see how powerful my message can be. I'm glad you're in my life.

To the Wiley team, especially Ruth Mills, for believing people would want to read what I wrote. And to my agent, Sheryl Fullerton, for helping this book become a reality.

To my mother, who always knew I'd be a writer someday. To my father, who hated the idea I would be a poor, starving writer and then I married one. (It didn't turn out so bad, did it, Dad?)

To my associate coaches: Deb, Joanne, Diane, and Chuck. You are always asking tough questions, which spurs me to develop even better ideas. Thank you for deciding to be a part of The JWC Group team. Your contribution is deeply appreciated.

To my husband, Steve. You spent your time editing my material, and you told me when my work was great and when it needed help. Your guidance on becoming a writer has made this work possible. What I'm deeply grateful for is your constant, never-ending support for who I am. I love you, baby.

To my clients, past and present. Your struggles, your successes, your failures, and your celebrations have been an inspiration. It is because of you that I strive to make more of my life each and every day.

And to you, the reader. Although we haven't met, we're somehow connected. I know you have much to teach me on this journey. Keep the faith. You can have the life you've always wanted to live.

ABOUT THE AUTHOR

Jennifer White is the founder and president of The JWC Group, a success coaching firm that helps high achievers create thriving careers and richly satisfying lives.

A nationally syndicated columnist, Jennifer is recognized as a leading authority on success, and she speaks to a wide variety of audiences on many of the topics you read in this book. She's appeared in *USA Today*, The *Washington Post*, *Entrepreneur Magazine*, and hundreds of other business publications.

Jennifer and her husband Steve live with their seven pets in Kansas City, Missouri. You can reach the author at her e-mail address: jencoach@successu.com.

ABOUT THE JWC GROUP

One thing I know about Work Less, Make More is that it's more than just a book. It's a new way of working and of living.

But I'm no fool. Change is hard, and it can be difficult, and sometimes you can't do it alone. Many people like to read all the books that tell them how to become more successful, but somehow they just don't apply what they're learning. Don't let that happen to you.

I've developed a variety of specific programs to help you integrate Work Less, Make More into your life. One of the best ways to integrate what you're learning is to stay in touch with me. I've set up an extensive web site to be your Work Less, Make More resource center. Go ahead and visit it at:

www.worklessmakemore.com.

You'll find a whole series of new information to help you along your success journey, including a free, weekly e-mail newsletter that's full of new ideas and strategies to help you work less and make more. Visit the site to subscribe.

If you're interested in hiring your own success coach, either individually or in a group setting, e-mail us at sales@successu.com or call my office at (800) 853-6218. We also conduct in-house training programs, keynote speeches, and executive coaching/consulting services. Call us. We want to hear from you.

The JWC Group
(800) 853-6218
jencoach@successu.com
www.worklessmakemore.com
www.jwcgroup.com

INDEX

INDEX

Change:
  in actions, 109–111
  impact of, 11–12
  in speaking behavior, 108–109
  in thinking behavior, 107–108
Charitable contributions,
    205–207
Chopra, Deepak, 206
Clothing, innovation and, 189
Clutter:
  elimination of (see Decluttering
    guidelines)
  impact of, 127–128
Coach, role of, 8
Co-leaders, 81
Color, in inspirational
    environment, 187
Commitment, duplication and,
    151
Communication skills, 88–89
Competition, 163
Compounding, 207–208
Conflict, 148–149
Connecting strategies, in power
    relationships, 219–221
Consumable products sales, 211
Courage, importance of, 15–16
Creative Day, 98
Creativity:
  believing in yourself, 180–182
  importance of, 177–179
  innovation and, 182
Critic, characteristics of, 36–37
Current clients, 73–74
Customers:
  classification of, 171–172
  focus on, 164–165, 171–172
  innovation and, 192
  loyal vs. satisfied, 164–165,
    174
  relationship with, 167–168,
    192 (see also Power
    relationships)

selling to, 211
value and, 162, 172–173

Deadlines:
  as motivation, 192–193
  procrastination and, 106–111
Debt management, 202–204
Decluttering guidelines, 128–131
Delegate, defined, 75–79
Delegation, benefits of, generally,
    131, 146–152
Disorganization, impact of, 128
Do It, Delegate It, Dump It
    philosophy, 130–131, 134
Duplication:
  benefits of, 145–146
  delegation, 146–152
  determining what to duplicate,
    152–154
  success of, 155–156
  using technology, 154–155

80/20 rule, 67–69, 88–89
Eliminate, defined, 75
E-mail, 133
Emotional fulfillment, 29
Employees, hiring strategies,
    146–152
Enthusiasm, 9
Environment, inspirational,
    186–189

Failure:
  benefits of, generally, 224–225
  dealing with, 114–115
  power relationship with,
    221–223
  success strategies and,
    223–224
Faxes, 134
Fear, dealing with, 15, 18
Fees, increasing, 200
Financial consultant, role of, 208

INDEX

6700586R0

Made in the USA
Lexington, KY
14 September 2010